Get Your People to Work Like They *Mean It!*

Get Your People to Work Like They *Mean It!*

Jean Blacklock
Evelyn Jacks

McGraw-Hill

New York   Chicago   San Francisco   Lisbon   London   Madrid   Mexico City
Milan   New Delhi   San Juan   Seoul   Singapore   Sydney   Toronto

The **McGraw·Hill** *Companies*

1 2 3 4 5 6 7 8 9 0   DOC/DOC   0 9 8 7 6

ISBN-13: 978-0-07-147053-7
ISBN-10:   0-07-147053-0

This publication is designed to provide accurate and authoritative information in regard to the subject matter covered. It is sold with the understanding that the publisher is not engaged in rendering legal, accounting, or other professional service. If legal advice or other expert assistance is required, the services of a competent professional person should be sought.

—From a Declaration of Principles Jointly Adopted by a Committee of the American Bar Association and a Committee of Publishers and Associations

McGraw-Hill books are available at special discounts to use as premiums and sales promotions, or for use in corporate training programs. For more information, please write to the Director of Special Sales, Professional Publishing, McGraw-Hill, Two Penn Plaza, New York, NY 10121-2298. Or contact your local bookstore.

 This book is printed on recycled, acid-free paper containing a minimum of 50% recycled de-inked paper.

*This book is dedicated to the millions of middle managers
in organizations of all kinds who tirelessly provide
the personal coaching and mentorship individuals need to succeed
and in doing so become leaders within their own right.*

CONTENTS

ACKNOWLEDGMENTS

We wish to acknowledge the insights of Mr. Russell May, President, Cypress Leadership, Inc., Executive Team Development, for his insights and observations stemming from a 30-year career in executive recruitment, which led us to many of our Real Life observations throughout this book.

We would also like to acknowledge the research assistance provided by Anne von Rosenbach and Cordell Jacks.

INTRODUCTION

For every leader out there, there is another story as to how he or she ended up in management, sometimes by design, often quite by accident. Yet the skills demanded of management in achieving results today have rarely been greater, with the stakes ever increasing, year over year. The speed of change has everyone working at a furious pace, but not always in tandem for the same results.

At the same time that everyone in the office, regardless of position, is bombarded with endless communications, 24/7—via e-mail, various handheld devices including cell and office phone, fax, and text messaging—we struggle to find thinking time to focus on what is important. Someone needs to manage the work–life balance that all employees want with today's realities and tomorrow's competitors. The company that succeeds at this will win— and winning requires strong middle management.

Never before has working with people been more important. One can have the best ideas coming from the most talented leaders, the most innovative work structures, and the most accurate forecasts and business plans, but without expert execution by the entire team, the company will not get the results it wants.

Expectations for financial results have radically changed over the past ten years, with analysts seeking improved productivity ratios every year. And whereas each of us who leads a business or business unit may have a credible explanation for our team's failure to achieve its plan, the market shows little sympathy to the chief executive officer who issues quarterly results below the financial analysts' targets. This pressure quickly finds its way to middle management.

In a leadership role, there are many things that we can blame when we don't get the results we want, chief among the scapegoats being an overly aggressive business plan and people on our team who "just don't get it!" Many times as we were writing this book, people we spoke with regaled us with their personal stories about leading individuals who seemed to have an overdeveloped sense of entitlement or an underdeveloped self-awareness. Others bemoaned the challenges of working with bright and talented individuals, many of whom are striving to be made an executive before age 30, dismissive of the company's "work–life policies."

The dilemma for the leader is that regardless of the aspirations of the individuals on the team, it is expected that better bottom line results will be delivered each year, at the same time as the manager implements the company's flexible human resource policies. Sometimes this can feel like an impossible task. Particularly when you take into account that today people can work anytime, anywhere. The corollary to this is that our customers can buy our products and services anytime, from anywhere! Management must consider new ways to lead and influence people to do the right things, the first time—as top quality is critical in our split-second reactions—in order to meet ever-increasing demands for productivity improvements.

This reality is further driven by increased annual demands from shareholders and the competitive demands of a global marketplace. No one individual can perform at the required pace, at least not for very long. *In fact, it's not about one person anymore—it's about the team!*

This is good news for the middle manager, who has reemerged as a significant asset. The quest is for better productivity results in a global marketplace filled with millions of potential new customers … if you "get this," and are a smart, enthusiastic, innovative, and energetic manager, yours is a golden future.

Back to the present, however, who is going to manage Julia's absenteeism due to her elderly mother's illness, and the enormous expertise gap left with Mason's sudden departure for the South Seas with his other postuniversity pals? Who will cope with Mary's lethargy as she puts in yet another year of tenured presence in anticipation of her husband's retirement? Who will put brilliant and advancement-impatient Shawna on the right track to ensure she doesn't self-destruct or leap to the competition? Who has the insight to persuade Ken to take a day off, away from his handheld devices, to avoid the burnout he is speeding into?

Just how do you get people to work like they mean it when "life" and work collide? How do you get them to shape up as individuals, pass off the right tasks to their team members at precisely the right time, and make decisions as a team? How do you create a team buzz, get people fully engaged with one another, and foster a culture so in tune with the marketplace and all its various stakeholders that together you can work on the leading edge—that is, proactively instead of reactively?

The answer is simple. If you are in middle management today, *you must have the personal confidence to lead a team with the commitment and passion to get the right results, every time.* That requires you to take on four main responsibilities in team building: (1) consistent role modeling from you; (2) the right work structure; (3) the right plan; and (4) the right people.

It is the organization that gets everyone on the team fully engaged in execution that will win. What's winning? In the short term, it's being on plan. But in the long term it's having a workplace that attracts top talent, fosters low staff turnover, and focuses on satisfied customers and clients who become your champions over time.

To be a great manager, you don't require an MBA, another degree, or more industry workshops. Whether you have "happened into management" or are there because of your professional training, it all boils down to how good you are at dealing with people issues and coaching a team over the finish line. And in this day-to-day guide to becoming a leading-edge middle manager, we'll show you how. We know that leading people is more art than science, requiring middle management to meet three essential goals:

1. Lead a group of unique people—*as a team*—to optimal performance, both in the short and the long term.
2. Bring out the best in each individual on the team.
3. Use intuitive intelligence to work effectively with the external community beyond the team.

To help you achieve these goals, we will challenge you to consider developing an operating structure and process from which you can better tap the valuable knowledge base of your employees. We will present you with an opportunity to review your personal focus and efforts around the all-important achievement of your plan. And finally, we will ask you to consider your responsibility to ensure that people on you team are presented with opportunities to do meaningful work and are fully engaged in it.

People who have a stake in the team's results are highly motivated and are rewarding to lead. But it takes skill, confidence and vision to successfully recruit, train, motivate, and retain them.

In Part 2 of this book, we present four special opportunities—key management issues you can approach in a leading-edge fashion. You'll be asked to consider your role in:

- Taking time for assessment and evaluation
- Preventing and addressing performance gaps
- Managing top performers
- Connecting your team to the big picture

Throughout this book we offer personal insights and real-life scenarios from experienced executives, human resource consultants, business owners, and leaders, to provide you with some new ideas on handling the issues that you face daily.

We hope that this book will make you think, will help you to personally win big in relation to your opportunities for advancement, and also will help you *to experience the energy that comes from leading great teams of people.*

Get Your People to Work Like They *Mean It!*

PART 1

THE
RESPONSIBILITIES
OF
LEADERSHIP

RESPONSIBILITY 1

YOU, THE LEADER

"When head and heart are working in cooperation ...
thought, word and deed are in harmony. This shows itself
as integrity and authenticity, and where there is authenticity
there is authentic power."

Ross Lawford,
The Quest for Authentic Power

Leadership → Results

Real Life

Whether you are a parent raising a child, a teacher educating someone else's child, or a manager responsible for leading a team toward a common goal, leadership is a formidable task. It requires a focused, accountable effort to persuade and compel others to willingly work with you. Although often rewarding and challenging, leadership is rarely easy. It requires commitment, resourcefulness, and the ability to listen, learn, and earn the trust of the team and others who rely on it. The days of "command and control" in the workplace are gone. The people on your team have an absolute ability to follow you or not. Sure, you have the title, and they need their jobs, but whether they choose to *follow* you, or simply to do what you tell them to do, are two entirely different choices, with different outcomes.

Your success as a leader depends on the choice they make. And a large part of that choice is driven by whether you are seen as *authentic*—confident in your skills and comfortable in your own skin. Authenticity is the key to effective leadership today.

All we really have as a leader is influence, and truly influential leaders are both inspiring and powerful. The question is whether you have a positive or negative influence in leading your team, whether they respect you, and therefore whether you succeed or fail in getting the results you want.

As a new middle manager, it is easy to get caught up in the trappings of leadership and sucked into a whirlwind of important meetings, crises, and flying e-mails. In the process, it is tempting to think that the new title and position place you in some rarefied space where you will be respected by your team "no matter what." People are usually careful to not show disrespect to their manager, and in fact, some individuals are exceptionally talented at hiding their real thoughts and opinions about the boss. *What differentiates successful leaders from average leaders is their ability to understand the behavioral and emotional issues around leadership and develop enduring relationships with people in their sphere of influence.*

IT'S ABOUT THE RELATIONSHIP

You must know yourself really well in order to master the behavioral and emotional issues that arise in leadership. Your first responsibility as a good leader is to think about your personal values, attributes, and behaviors. Are these characteristics deserving of your team's respect?

There are two ways to get results: in the short term and in the long term. In the short term, you may be able to get people to do things by raising your voice or making threats, creating a culture of compliance in which people are externally rewarded by things like their salary. But over time, really succeeding with your team requires that you earn your team's respect, and more importantly, earn the commitment of the members, *so that every person on the team is inspired and self-motivated.*

Your team is very perceptive about who is doing what in the management ranks, and that includes you. You can't be a dishonest, nasty person in your personal life and expect to be an upstanding, well-respected leader in your work life. It doesn't happen like that. Your team will inevitably come to recognize the real you, and they will decide whether to follow your lead, or simply to fake compliance.

In Responsibility 1, we will look at the new traits required of managers in increasingly fast-paced business environments that feature increased pressures for productivity and profitability. *In demand are leaders who can attract and retain a team; carefully listen to individuals to better analyze opportunities, challenges, and threats; and persuade, motivate, and inspire the entire team to get behind the results required.*

Are you trustworthy and transparent? Do you command the respect of your team by being both "caring" and "accountable"? Do people want to work for you? These are the traits sought by recruiters and boards, traits established over time, with consistent performance on your part. Yet there is more required. On one hand, it is essential that you are the genuine article, a person who has integrity and sufficient humility to recognize that connecting with the people on your team is the only hope you have of success. On the other hand, all the empathy and warm fuzzies in the world mean nothing if your team doesn't make its plan. As the team's leader, you must accept that you are accountable for rallying the troops in a successful planning and implementation process so that the team's goals can be achieved.

In short, reputations for performance mastery and personal integrity are *earned* day by day.

Chapter 1

FORGET THE BIG TITLE—WHO ARE YOU, REALLY?

"Middle managers are . . . the chief community builders . . . the main trustees of the integrity and moral practices of the firm. They are its moral and intellectual spine."
Michael Novak, *Business as a Calling*

Real Life

It is tempting to see your job in management as a very complicated activity. By its nature, a leadership role is complex: a business of some sort to be run, business targets and goals to achieve, a few or many team members to manage, and so on. Viewed with the broadest lens, leadership brings with it a lot of moving parts and spinning plates. And yet if we step back and consider what the job of a manager really is, the answer can be quite simple.

You are the steward of your company's resources. In taking responsibility for an assignment (often in the form of a business plan to be achieved), you must possess the skills to analyze the assignment accurately so that you can figure out a successful way to achieve the desired results and develop a team that can make it happen. Or stated another way: *Whittle the expectations down to manageable pieces and leverage each member of the team up to his or her optimal performance.* To do this well, in the context of today's demanding marketplace, you must be able to demonstrate success not only as an individual but also within the context of your ability to recruit, retain, and inspire a team of talented people. This requires a deep understanding of your personal mission, within your own "big picture" and an ability to reflect objectively on your results.

When you know yourself, you will know how to lead.

GREAT LEADERS DO IMPORTANT WORK

And in so doing they get great results. But to achieve these, your management career requires your full commitment to your role. There needs to be careful planning, astute recruitment, ongoing communication, and detailed execution. *But the real success in leadership lies in your ability to compel people to work with you willingly toward a common goal.* This in turn requires self-awareness: an understanding of both your reasons for wanting to lead people and your personal strengths and weaknesses.

Poor leaders neither reflect on their personal motivations nor possess the ability or desire to see themselves as others do. In fact, they often are role players. Russell May, President of Cypress Leadership Inc., a company focused on executive team development, puts it this way: "There are two types of people in this world: those who are someone and those who want to be someone."

The alternative to being a transparent authentic person is obviously to try to be someone else, which leads to role-playing and insecurity. Insecure leaders tend not to invite input on their decisions. Emanating from their insecurity is a raft of counterproductive behaviors which provide obstacles to results. Everything is a battle. They have a tendency to be defensive when challenged, they generally do not like or invite input or ideas from others, and when they do receive them, they either won't acknowledge the source or refuse to consider and employ those ideas.

Good leaders, on the other hand, recognize that to be a "leader," and not only a "manager," they must be aware and respectful of their impact on others.

WHO ARE YOU?

When it comes to a professional vocation, particularly in management, you have the choice to find a job in which you show up, don your uniform (literally or as a figure of speech), work away until the day is done, and then return to your "real life" at the end of the day. The corollary of this choice is that your hobbies, relationships, and activities outside of your livelihood truly define you.

In contrast, a leadership role requires you to reflect on who you are and the values and personal characteristics that equip you to lead others.

Much more important than what you do or say is who and what you are. Ralph Waldo Emerson made this point succinctly: "What you are shouts so loudly in my ears I can't hear what you say."

Think of your own reaction upon meeting someone new. Whether in a social setting, at your son's hockey practice, or in a work meeting, upon the first introduction, you are running your perceptions of the new person through the conscious or unconscious system that has served you well in the past. You are making inferences, assumptions, and even judgments within minutes. The people you lead similarly assess you, and in that situation (team members' views of the manager), it is usually judgment in the most pointed form.

DO YOU HAVE CHARISMA?

One way in which leaders influence others is seen in politics. It is sometimes referred to as "charisma," but that word seems to lack some element of the tremendous sway that certain elected leaders hold over the electorate. Our purely anecdotal observation is that this form of influence can compel us to vote for an individual who doesn't even endorse well-articulated beliefs, or whose tenets do not line up with what a voter has previously believed. We saw this with "Trudeaumania" in Canada where people with quite conservative views nevertheless jumped on the liberal bandwagon for a time. In the United States, John F. Kennedy and Bill Clinton similarly benefitted at the polls with their tremendous personal charisma. One manager who had met President Clinton at a small function described his entrance into the room as simply "sucking all the air out." We cannot and would not suggest that "sucking all the air out" of the boardroom on Monday morning is the impact you should strive for in your work; besides being an unlikely feat, we assume it would quickly wear thin on the team.

The Effect of Charismatic Leaders on Team Success

- Sensitivity to member needs
- Sensitivity to the environment
- Personal risk-taking
- Vision and articulation
- Performing unconventional behavior

Source: J.A. Conger and R.N. Kanungo,
Charismatic Leadership in Organizations,
Sage Publications, Thousand Oaks, CA, 1998.

Charismatic leaders can in fact provide a toxic environment, however. Sander Rubin, a chairman of American Mensa, makes an important point in this regard:

> There is no good that, taken to excess, is not also evil. The trouble starts at the top, not the bottom . . . I have consciously rejected two techniques of government, the charismatic and the legalistic. Charismatic leadership induces the consent of the governed through emotional appeal. It is virtually self-evident that such a source of consent is inconsistent with both the exercise of intelligence and the presumption of equality. As a practical matter, this kind of government stirs the resentment and opposition of many and limits the scope of the society to the vision, or lack of it, of its leader.

(From the 1973 *Mensa Annual Report*. See http://www.dcn. davis.ca.us/~sander/mensa/rep73a.html.)

So we conclude that charisma, although important, is only one element of steller leadership.

CHECK YOUR EGO

We all have egos. Some are healthy, some are not. If you choose to lead, and if it is your goal to hone your calling into great leadership, it is important that you understand the health of your own ego and its effect on the team. *Ego* is defined in dictionaries as self-awareness; *egotism*, as conceit. Egocentric people tend to view everything in relation to themselves as opposed to the group.

Some Personal Insights: On Fragile Egos

Egoless leadership can be counterproductive, too. On the opposite end of the spectrum are people who are so humble and selfless, that recognition rarely comes their way, unless it is by the fact that others enable it. This can in fact be empowering for the team, but in the absence of reciprocity, create an imbalance which also is unhealthy. These people may, in fact also be poor leadership candidates if their ego is not sufficiently present to stand up for the team, its mission, its value, and what's right in terms of the structure and plan. Many companies have fallen when new charismatic leaders, with self-interests, wrestle the company away from the egoless. In both cases, these are leaders whose values are not firmly enough established, with the result that they can be easily swayed into the dark side of unintended results.

When you take on the responsibility of leadership, you must stay firmly rooted in your values and principles and know what obstacles you must overcome in order to lead your team—in as straight a line as possible—to the results you want.

To help you think about your ego and its effect on others, consider John Maxwell's quote, "The first step to leadership is servanthood." And in a similar vein, Robert Greenleaf defined the "servant leader" as an individual who emphasizes connections between self and organization, between listening and understanding, and between language and imagination. Servant leadership places the leader at the nexus, rather than at the pinnacle, of change.

We believe that the key to becoming an influential and inspirational leader starts with having a strong confidence in your own abilities. But before you can achieve such confidence, you must first understand your personal values and goals, and you must have a personal vision.

HAVE A VISION

People like to be around those with a personal vision, especially if they can integrate that vision into the team's work and engage people in it. By exhibiting personal strength and independence of thought, you are more likely to be seen as inspirational, intuitive, resourceful—not just another manager. *The ability to know and trust in oneself is a key trait of effective and influential leadership.*

Traits of Influential Leaders

- **Accountable:** "The price of greatness is responsibility." *Winston Churchill.*
- **Charitable:** "The man of wealth becomes the mere trustee and agent for his poorer brethren." *Andrew Carnegie, 1868.*
- **Creative:** "Innovation is a form of change. Leaders can help unusual people produce innovations—even if it's not out of thin air. But leading creative people in this age of diverse work arrangements and electronic relationships requires leaders themselves to be thoughtfully innovative. The secret, I believe, lies in how individual

leaders in a great variety of settings make room for people with unusual and creative gifts and temporarily become followers themselves." (*Source: Max De Pree, Leadership Is an Art, New York: Doubleday/Currency Books, revised edition, 2004.*)

- **Community-Focused:** "Why are we here? A group of people get together and exist as an institution we call a company so that they are able to accomplish something collectively that they could not accomplish separately—they make a contribution to society, a phrase that sounds trite, but is fundamental." *David Packard, Hewlett-Packard.*

- **Frugal:** "Be gentle and you can be bold; be frugal and you can be liberal; avoid putting yourself before others and you can become a leader among men." *Lao Tzu.*

- **Goal-Oriented:** "Successful people are not afraid of challenging goals. In fact—clear, specific goals that produce a lot of challenge—tend to produce the best results! Coaches that have the courage to tell the truth "upfront" and challenge leaders in goal-setting can go beyond being "highly paid friends." *Marshall and Kelly Goldsmith.*

- **Knowledgeable:** "Leadership and learning are indispensable to each other." *John F. Kennedy.*

- **Passionate:** "It is a real thrill to try to give the small investor—of which our companies are mainly comprised—as good a job as the big man gets." *Edward Crosby Johnson II, founder, Fidelity Investments.*

- **Persistent:** "I have not failed. I've just found 10,000 ways that won't work." *Thomas Alva Edison.*

- **Principaled:** "For those who desire to be moral and credible leaders, they must demonstrate virtuous leadership in speech and actions, publicly and privately, 24 hours a day. No leader will ever become a spotless moral paragon.

And yet, each must be committed to doing what it takes to do what is right. What a leader does in private does matter and will ultimately establish or undermine the credibility of his or her influence. The motivation of the leader must be the message of his or her entire life rather than the method by which that person hides his or her secrets." *John Hawkins, president of Leadership Edge, Inc.*

VISION AND TEAM CULTURE

In their desire to be respected by their team, some managers underestimate the importance of their personal behavior, attributes, and attitudes. They believe that the culture of the larger organization is somehow imparted to the team, for better or worse, with minimal impact possible from the immediate manager. In our experience, this is not true.

Although your fundamental, absolutely essential task as a manager is to deliver the results that will lead to the enterprise's ongoing viability, this can only be achieved by maximizing the personal contribution of each team member. In turn, an individual's drive to succeed is increased exponentially if he or she buys into the leader as the "boss," not by title, *but out of respect.* If the leader is personally influential to the team, through his or her leadership, the strategic vision of the company can most successfully be executed by the team members.

The result is enhanced productivity because people are *internally,* rather than externally, motivated by the leader.

BUILDING "PRESENCE"

Some people have presence; some don't. It's not about looks, dress, or etiquette—although we agree that a consistent professional appearance can be influential. And, it's not about being a "vanilla flavored" leader.

How can one be comfortable with one's own personal style and personality, and a yet exude a presence suitable to the current leadership role or, ideally, one which is a level or two more senior. Where does such a presence come from?

Consider John Baldoni's perspective from "The Presence of Leadership":

> Just as leadership is a reflection of earned authority, leadership presence, which enhances the leadership moment, is derived from the support of others. Leadership presence is a necessary attribute of leadership. You can define it as the presence of authority imbued with a reason to believe. What matters to us most is authenticity. That cannot be faked, but it can be amplified. Leadership is about the other person. Get it by projecting authority, listening, holding people accountable, appreciating what people do by showing up.

Some Personal Insights: On Following a Leader

Following is optional. There are lots of smart, knowledgeable people who never make it to the top of their field, who are passed by for promotions or who lack influence and power. People have to like you, as well as respect you for those things that set you apart, in order to want to work with you, or follow your lead. A good rule of thumb: If I enjoy lunch with you, if you can capture my curiosity, provide me with a new insight, gain my respect in terms of your own pride in your personal accomplishments, and help me understand why you are interested in working with me, I probably have a reason to consider working with or for you. Do I want to be on your team? This is entirely my personal choice, and every leader should remember this.

UNCLUTTER YOUR LIFE

You need to manage yourself before you can manage others. You must be regarded as a credible, respected leader who focuses on the things that matter to the team's success. Without respect and credibility, your efforts to build a dynamic and tell-it-like-it-is culture in which good employees become great ones, is doomed from the start. *Beyond knowing yourself, you must manage yourself on a day-to-day basis within a reflective process.*

One of the great difficulties in leading a team today is the demands that encroach upon your quality thinking time. At work, it is paramount that you stay focused on where you and your team are headed, on a daily basis. You can easily complicate your role as a leader by doing things such as:

- Agreeing to spend time in good activities that are not directly related to the main goals (confusing "doing" with "achieving")
- Micromanaging: refusing to delegate tasks that someone else can and should do, or refusing to get out of the way to let them do it
- Failing to consistently follow up on progress
- Balking at making tough decisions such as standing up to senior management on behalf of the team or parting ways with a disruptive team member

We hasten to underscore that laserlike focus on the team's plan doesn't require you to become one of those harried-looking people who never returns e-mails or phone calls and is always running late. Nor does focus require ruthless "prioritization" (please save us from corporate jargon!), editing from your schedule each and every item and event that appears irrelevant on its surface. Leaders who choose (and it is a choice) to be harried, fail to return calls and e-mails in a day or two, never show up at the birthday cake time in the boardroom, and rarely have time to just chat in the lunchroom simply don't get the big picture. Even assuming you are focused on the right things, if you ignore too much "minutiae," you may be making a mistake. In adopting such a "very important person" persona, you confuse your immediate pressing projects with the ongoing success of the team.

On the other hand, by clogging your schedule and cluttering up your mental or physical space with all of the nonessential calls, e-mails, articles, books, letters, and meeting requests that come your way, you and your team can soon be working at a furious pace and getting nowhere. The ongoing success of the team requires that you know when to slow down and take time just to "chat" and when to be ruthlessly focused, demanding, and driven.

BE FIRM AND FRIENDLY

Your job as a leader is to never get too far from the main responsibilities of understanding the team's objectives and creating the team to achieve it. It is also your job to sit back, reflect, and make sure everyone is pointed in the right direction to achieve desired results. Without that focus, it is very hard to have the confidence to be upfront and clear, telling people what needs to be told, and when they need to hear it.

RELATING TO THE DEMOGRAPHICS

Do you lead the young or the old? You may encounter special challenges with each demographic you work with. Take the leadership of younger workers—those born after 1975—for example. This demographic segment resists conformity even as they enter their thirties; they are unlikely to be impressed or influenced by leaders who cannot develop (or even condone) some degree of personal flair or style.

In other words, there is a shift in society toward the expression of one's personality that appears to be entrenched. If you are able and willing to let your personality show in an appropriate way in your leadership role, you will undoubtedly be seen as a more progressive, open, and flexible leader. These attributes will assist you in engaging those people on your team who were not raised to act, dress, or think like everybody else.

GIVING IT YOUR "ALL"

Some people live as if their personal and professional lives are separate and distinct from each other, as if one were a means for the other. However, this is not possible if you are to become an effective leader, as it is difficult to be at cross purposes in your personal and professional lives. *The essence of leadership is that to be successful at it, you must be worthy of influencing others, motivating them to show up to work every day and give to the organization the very best that they have to give, not because they get a paycheck or because you tell them to, but because they respect your leadership.*

If you truly want to lead and influence people by establishing relationships that permit you to tell the truth, and therefore get the results you want, then you simply must become a "student" of leadership. You must observe every day the impact that you and other leaders have in situations, assessing for yourself what works and what doesn't, and which of your personal values, views, attitudes, and attributes requires another look.

In short, *great leaders make an impact because they lead their teams within the context of their whole lives.*

SUMMING UP

What is your vision for your own personal leadership? For your team? For the company? It helps to have anchor points—personal and team vision statements that can help bring you and the team back to the basics when challenges arise. In developing your personal mission statement, consider:

- What motivates me?
- What do I value?
- What keeps me up at night?
- What am I good at?
- What am I *not* good at?
- Do I like myself?
- What do I fear?
- Am I capable of embracing and delivering a vision?

- Can I inspire others to follow me?
- How can I earn their trust?
- Is my personal life in balance with my career?

In preparing a team mission statement, consider the following elements for team success.

1. **Ethical Framework:** What are the things I need to do on a daily basis to create trust between myself and my team members?
2. **Cultural Framework:** What are the values and beliefs the team will operate under?
3. **Commitment to Knowledge Culture:** How will we share knowledge to encourage the new or less experienced? How will we embrace new learning opportunities to encourage risk-taking and build the organization?
4. **Shared Objectives:** How do we achieve success together by integrating our efforts?
5. **Results Framework:** How do we define results?

Chapter 2

EVERY CEO IS
SOMEBODY'S KID

Real Life

As a leader, you are a professional change manager. Your skills must include the ability to help people move from one changing situation to another—both in their jobs and sometimes in their personal lives.

While some people expect current conditions to last indefinitely, it is unrealistic in either our personal or professional lives to assume that people, things, or situations will remain unchanged for long. Health, wealth, and success—we all know that these conditions are fleeting. Because many people have difficulty accepting and dealing with change, as a leader you must be very comfortable with change, even initiating change at times, and must be able to help your team move through it with ease.

To be good at this, it is important that you first have the ability to manage change in your own life, and see where leadership fits into the big picture for you.

WHAT IS THE ROLE OF LEADERSHIP IN YOUR WHOLE LIFE?

It may sound quite lofty to think about leadership as part of your "whole life," but most effective leaders do not separate work from the rest of life. This approach, by the way, absolutely does not mean you need to be a slave to small technology tools throughout your daughter's piano concert! In fact, we mean quite the opposite.

Why is a separation of your leadership role from your whole life impossible? Because we can influence others to act only if they see something in us that makes them want to follow us. That "something" can include your proven ability to get results for the company or your success as an entrepreneur, but in and of itself, that is not enough. Eventually there will be a bump in the road and at that point, people will stand by you only if you have influenced them in some other way.

Therefore, it is important to reflect on your personal leadership in the context of the rest of your life. One way to do so is to consider the concept of the *I-Chart*. This illustration is particularly helpful for those who are impatient for leadership roles (warming up on the sidelines in careful preparedness) as well as those who are reluctant to give up the reins of leadership (the winding down years away from the fray, properly managed, can often result in your most meaningful work as an individual and a mentor).

THE I-CHART

As well as giving some consideration to your physical presence, demeanor, and style, it is useful to view leadership in the context of life stages. Talented younger managers who feel disengaged within larger corporate organizations should consider the accompanying I-Chart. It is a way to understand the leadership process as it relates to your whole life.

This snapshot also allows senior and junior leaders to think and chat about their evolving leadership roles—and the challenge of life balance that comes with these roles—in three stages:

1. The warming-up years before your first leadership role.
2. The years of engagement when you step up to lead people.

3. The winding-down phase, and retirement years, when you have the opportunity to entrench your life's work in the form of teaching, mentoring, or philanthropy.

Remember, the straight line between your starting and finish lines—birth and death—is finite, and we each have only so much time on earth to make it all happen. Therefore, understanding where you are in relation to your whole life often can help you prioritize the many responsibilities you may be juggling, now or in the future.

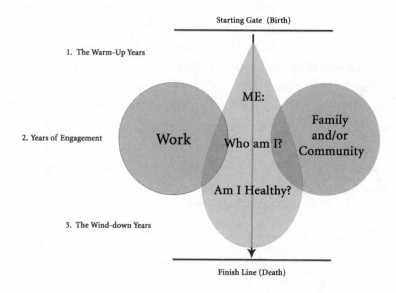

The I-Chart can help you explain the process of advancement and influence to impatient young business school graduates who seek instant gratification relating to their need for making a personal impact in their work. You can remind those people on the team who are new to their careers that influential leaders are not born; they evolve as a by-product of trust, *which is earned.* Every person must put in his or her time to take the stage of full engagement.

When it comes to influential leadership opportunities, young people with high potential should be encouraged to relax: the question for them is not whether full engagement in a leadership role will ever occur, but rather, when. The questions they must ask *themselves* are: Will I be ready? And, what am I doing now, in the warm-up period, to prepare myself for leading others?

It is clear that in the leadership engagement period we are most challenged in terms of balance, with the circles of responsibility varying in size depending on the circumstances (the younger the family, the larger that circle is at the expense of work and personal development). For those very reasons it is most important for those who find themselves on either side of this engagement period in life to enjoy their current place within the lifeline. Those who are warming up should do so with vigor and enthusiasm, in anticipation of what is to come. Those who are winding down should embrace the opportunity to really have an impact—and perhaps do their best life's work—when they are out of the direct fray of engagement.

It is also clear from this chart that ultimately, there is only one party responsible for managing the Me Circle—and that's You. While work and family obligations clearly impact your journey, in the end it's *your* lifeline.

TAKE THE TIME TO WARM UP

If the respect of your team is important, and most people think that it is, then the importance of the future leader's experiences *before* first managing a team of people can't be overstated. These experiences also provide the needed credibility when it comes time to provide feedback, both positive and negative. Just as a lean, muscular body gives a personal trainer a good part of his or her authority in laying out a weight-training program for clients, direction and guidance from a respected and credible person with a track record of success carries greater weight with her team.

Not surprisingly, then, common advice to recent graduates from even the most prestigious business schools is to *get some experience, in order to be credible.* The best type of experience is open for debate but the fact is that it is less about the type of experience and more about finding ways to assume responsibility for project success, whether in a business setting or otherwise, where the work requires more than simply your individual work and effort. Inevitably these types of projects become "leadership opportunities" because successful completion requires you to bring together a group of people to work together for a common goal, which is the fundamental essence of leadership.

In later years, when you apply for more formal leadership jobs, your project experience will be influential in a decision to hire you and will give you the ability to discuss those attributes of leadership that you developed. The informal type of leadership mentioned here will not always suffice, but it will certainly set the candidate apart from those who have achieved great marks and done well in a technical role but have never demonstrated even a desire to influence others to succeed in a joint undertaking.

Some Personal Insights About Environments and Parameters

When the freedom to learn and practice is matched with high standards, you get great individual and team results. Add a fence to that and you get a comfort zone attractive to top talent. Despite the fact that many in authority are uncomfortable setting standards of accountability, clear parameters provide a sense of the immediate environment for everyone as well as the discipline to work within that framework and to meet expectations that are not overwhelming.

When given a bar to meet, most people will want to meet or exceed it. High performers will always want to contribute more and the leader must encourage and be responsive to that desire, or else the best talent will soon look beyond their current environment. People outside your team will see your group as an environment in which to learn, grow, and prepare for their next new environment.

BALANCE WITH FULL ENGAGEMENT

Once engaged in a leadership career, it is worthwhile to keep your particular life stage in mind for two reasons. First, whether or not your stage of life is going to have a meaningful impact on your professional work (it may not), you need to be aware of its potential impact on members of your team.

For example, perhaps you lost your parents early in life so the responsibility for aging parents is not a life stage you will experience. Other colleagues will, however, and therefore the demands of caring for elderly parents are a consideration, a reality of a life stage that may or may not affect you personally, but could affect your team. Too often leaders are caught off guard by requests for leaves or more flexible work arrangements, when, if they had been attuned to the demands of different life stages, these requests could be anticipated as a possibility during the work planning process.

Second, a single-minded focus on only work has reached its peak as an attribute which commands admiration and respect and is likely on the wane. Although once working never-ending hours was perhaps an influential model, it now seems to be a point of dismay and disbelief in the people who work for and with such leaders. In fact, the newer generation—the one that comfortably and confidently follows its own heart—is most influenced by the executive who is grounded in a full life, complete with families or close friends, community activities, volunteer work, and other personal goals and aspirations.

You may be thinking that none of this applies to your "sweatshop" company or firm. That may be true in its present state, but presumably you are in a leadership role in that company and thus able to effect changes.

RECOGNIZE THE TIME TO WIND DOWN

The "sidelines" are really anything; but our upbringing, education, and work experience that precede a leadership role each exert considerable influence on the abilities we bring to our lifetime of relationships. Similarly, goals and aspirations about our postcareer years will shape not only the financial expectations we have of our career but should also provide us with perspective and context: especially if we are not defined by our titles or current position. *It is a fundamental part of the effective leader's self-awareness to care and think about life overall, not just his or her aspirations for the next career transfer.*

Some Personal Insights on Life-Cycle Change

In the absence of an understanding of the I-Chart, there is no plan for self-actualization. This, in fact, is a very sad waste of potential for influential mentorship and one that we have seen many times in the depression and even death of our most dynamic leaders who cannot envision life or identities outside of work.

The I-Chart is a useful tool in helping your team members evolve in and out of leadership roles within their personal lifelines, and the chart can help put the company's role in the management of life balance into perspective.

PERSONAL AND COMPANY LIFE CYCLES REQUIRE INSIGHTFUL LEADERSHIP

Leaders are professional change managers; their skill sets are unique to assisting others in moving from one changing condition to the next. The ability to manage oneself and lead others with courage and conviction through life-cycle and career change has much to do with how we were raised and our individual perspective on the temporary nature of the current state. As the old saying goes, change will either be forced upon us or managed by us. Your perspective on change will help you help your team members cope with their own life-cycle issues, or the life-cycle changes occurring in your company. If you want to be in a position to help your team members, both younger and older than yourself, understand that change management requires introspection. While most people expect current conditions to last indefinitely and often take youth, health, relationships, position, success, and harmony for granted, we really know that these conditions are temporary. Because people have difficulty accepting and dealing with change, it helps for leaders to develop a perspective on moving from one life cycle to another and how to cope successfully—that is, with a minimum of stress—with the unexpected.

SUMMING UP

Here are some questions to consider for successful life-cycle change management for yourself, your family, and your organization.

For Self

- Do I have a process for understanding my fears and therefore my choices?
- Can I envision my life after change?
- What value systems will guide my decisions for moving forward?
- What is negotiable, what is not?
- What do I need to do to prepare for the change?
- What resources can I draw on?
- If change is forced upon me, have I equipped myself with an emergency reserve—of time, connections and money?

For Self and Family

- Have we discussed the possibility of change and its effect on our family unit?
- What are our individual expectations in transitioning into change?
- Do we understand our strengths and weaknesses if change is forced upon us?
- Is our family prepared today to cope with dramatic change due to job loss, illness, or other unexpected circumstances?

At Work and in Our Careers

- Is change at work in harmony with my values?
- Who will I turn to for the best information in times of change?
- How will I evaluate the best time to stay or go?
- How will I integrate my career and financial requirements with the effect of change on my family and my health?

Chapter 3

YOU CAN LEAD...
BUT YOU CAN'T HIDE

Real Life

In any performance, it is important to understand your audience ... for most middle managers that's their team on one side and their boss on the other. On a day-to-day basis, some leaders act as if no matter what they do, they are immune from being assessed, critiqued, or evaluated by their teams. How untrue! As a leader you are under significant daily scrutiny by those above and below you in position and responsibility, and this affects your ability to execute. In fact, your team may know more about the "real you" than you do. Just how well do you relate to your team members? How well do you know each individual and his or her family?

It is to you alone that the team looks for their motivation and direction, especially at times when things are not going very well. In changing environments, which may include downsizing and consolidations as well as the normal pressure to meet profitability targets, it is your personal leadership style in relation to individual and team dynamics that will ultimately impact results.

Even in good times, the team looks to you for its energy and motivation. As the leader, it is up to you to help people:

1. Make an impact or a difference
2. Make decisions on their own
3. Feel recognized and appreciated for their contribution

FORGE RIGHT IN

Time and again, leaders undergoing 360-degree feedback assessments are surprised at their team's perceptivity about those "hidden" habits and traits that are not so secret after all. This is particularly important in an entrepreneurial environment. Business founders—who have the vision for the company and drive its creation and growth, often through difficult start-ups highlighted by lean years—are conditioned to think that the success of the business is "all about them." One of the biggest issues in the failure of family business succession is the ego of the owner and his or her inability to engage a succession team.

However, the scrutiny of the leader by team members is part of what makes leadership interesting. Many people these days search for meaning in their lives and in their work. A manager of people does not need to look too far to find meaning if that manager chooses to interpret his or her leadership role broadly as a means to positively influence others, to make them better than they were before, and to bring a number of disparate people together into a productive team. It is only because people observe you in these ways that you have any ability to influence them at all, to help you and the team get the results you and the company want.

This scrutiny is difficult, and requires that you have an open mind to judgments about your work as well as your personal relationships on the job. It is no wonder then, that despite academic, experiential, and personal successes, some new leaders have trouble transitioning their personal achievements into team successes. This requires time, the ability to take risks, and the courage to expose oneself to experiences with the team and the individuals on it.

PUT INFLUENTIAL LEADERSHIP INTO PRACTICE

There are many examples of influential and inspirational leadership around you daily. Try to find them not just in observing your bosses but in observing your team members, too. Think about them when you have a moment. Here are some examples we have come across in our own circles of influence.

Do As I Do

John, an executive vice president of a large national company, skied in the mountains with his young family every weekend. Joanna, a young entrepreneurial director came to the company after selling her small business. She was used to working 18-hour days and dealing with hundreds of details every week, at the expense of her personal time. She learned from John that the very best thing for the organization was delegation of the details by the leader, as appropriate, so that he could do his primary work—strategic thinking. He became, through his actions, her role model for professional focus and personal balance.

Simplicity Is Key

Bruce, a new senior vice president appointed to lead the retail and commercial division of a bank, joined a meeting of one of the divisional leadership teams to introduce himself. Responsible for many important aspects of running the division, he sat down at the table and simply said, "Hi, I'm Bruce, and I'm a salesman." In that simple sentence, he conveyed the most important task in his senior role, which was making sure that every day, every person in his division had something to sell and sold it.

Do the Right Thing

A senior person described the executive vice president for whom she worked in the most glowing terms—what a strong leader he is, how she hopes to be on his team for a long time, and so on. When asked why, the first example she gave was that he attended her mother's funeral. What does that possibly have to do with business and getting the results required in today's competitive workplace? Logically, nothing of course, but in reality, it meant everything to the individual and to her desire to do her work effectively.

In short, the hectic and harried approach to leading a team ignores the subtle elements to the main priorities that we have mentioned, specifically, focus on the plan and building a team. While there are indeed many meetings that can be skipped, as the barrage of demands and requests for your time come in, there are subtle elements that are essential: making a connection, courtesy and class, humility, and diligence and efficiency.

CONNECTION

So you don't have time to join in on the wedding shower or have lunch in the staff lunch room once in a while. Nor do you sit down and talk to the assistant who has nothing to do with sales and certainly isn't going to directly influence this year's bottom line one bit. You need to reconsider what it means to be a leader and think beyond the team that directly reports to you. The more senior you become, the more essential it will be to remember the cliché, "the speed of the leader is the speed of the team," with "speed" being replaceable by any noun.

As the leader of a group, the people at every level of the team need a connection with you and the managers that you lead, and as touchy feely as it may sound, that needs to be an emotional, personal connection rather than a logical connection.

The following example demonstrates this point:

> Jane's productivity as an inbound sales representative—a job she has held successfully for 12 years—is being affected by her husband's heart condition. She has missed three days of work in the

last two weeks and her concentration is poor. We are not getting the results we want.

The Wrong Move. To ignore it, or reprimand Jane.
The Consequence. You could lose Jane, a valuable effective employee and face the prospect of having to hire and train a new person, a costly commitment of time and money.

The Right Move. To invite Jane to discuss the problem, and her thoughts on potential solutions that are right for her, her family, and her team, for the short and long term.
The Consequence. You may be able to settle on a temporary sabbatical or flex time to deal with the situation, thereby accommodating her needs and binding her loyalties even closer to you and the company, while you minimize time and costs by hiring temporary help.

COURTESY AND CLASS

You simply must respond to the influx of requests (calls, e-mails, letters, and invitations) in a timely, honest manner. E-mails or calls can often be returned personally in under 30 seconds, even if only to say that a more fulsome response will come later or by an assistant or other team member who you know represents you well and to whom the request can be appropriately delegated. Why wait to do that? Do it when you listen to the call or get the e-mail. And don't commit to anything—lunch, completion of a report, a speech—if you have no intention of following up or doing a great job. Your mother was right; actions do speak louder than words.

The following example illustrates this point:

Bob, a busy senior executive, was provided the opportunity to sit in on an idea incubation meeting with a junior management team over lunch.

The Wrong Move. Bob fails to acknowledge the event.
The Consequence. The junior team feels their work is unimportant, and that management does not care. As a result,

innovation and productivity is stifled and employees are tempted to look for the next opportunity for recognition elsewhere.

The Right Move. Bob attends the meeting and the next day sends over a thank-you note, expressing his personal gratitude for the opportunity to listen to the presentation, taking the time to itemize the specific high points of the presentation for him and its potential for the company or its stakeholders.

The Consequence. Employees are impressed by this respectful behavior by such a busy man, which exponentially drives loyalty, innovation, and productivity by the employees to the benefit of the company and its stakeholders. In an electronic world with split-second messaging, there are few gestures as heartfelt and meaningful as a personal handwritten note from a team leader.

HUMILITY

Lightening up once in a while is directly related to your focus on maximizing the team because it makes you human, and people want to work for human beings! Regardless of your seniority, spending time once in a while just being relaxed and enjoying "the moment" with your team is rarely a waste. In addition to showing your humanity where is the rule book which decrees that the need for coffee breaks and time-outs diminish in direct relation to career advancement? Maybe there is no such rule book; perhaps we simply lose sight of our own needs a bit or overestimate our personal importance. Successful leaders almost always look after themselves, recognizing that success doesn't have to be hard, and that every day doesn't have to be jam-packed with important meetings to be called productive.

The following example demonstrates this point:

Ryan, the new technical analyst, and his assistant Ellen have been working on a new template that will assist the team in national communications with Internet clients. This has been a work in progress that is now ready to launch. It will save hours of phone and e-mail time for every team member, most of whom, however, will not be familiar with the new technology. Integration could be a problem.

The Wrong Move. To ignore the significance of the innovation and fail to leverage it into the organizational structure.
The Consequence. Ryan and Ellen's work will not be integrated to the degree it should. This is wasteful of time and resources and will affect Ryan and Ellen's commitment to future projects.

The Right Move. Take a formal time-out to champion the achievement, and allow Ryan and Ellen time to explain how the project will simplify efforts and help the team better achieve results.
The Consequence. Individual and team leadership opportunities that build and grow the company.

DILIGENCE AND EFFICIENCY

Use spare minutes to your benefit. Efficiency has received a bad reputation in recent years, and we agree that being highly efficient at the wrong tasks is not very effective. However, there are two good reasons why, in the quest to keep focused, you should consider the strategy of using the spare minute efficiently.

First, there will be times each day and maybe whole days, when you are tired. It may not be your best time of day or maybe you just had a late night. Regardless of the reason, try doing some of the little, easy things in those times that might otherwise not get done at all: a quick e-mail to say hello to someone you met at a recent banquet or a card to congratulate a salesperson for a great month. It is surprising how often doing something small and easy will refresh and renew one's energy, sufficient even to move onto a bigger and arguably more important task. The important thing, we find, is to "do something" when energy flags.

The second reason to use minutes efficiently is that realistically, leaders only get time bites some days, and if you don't take advantage of the gap between the meeting that ends at 2 and the one that starts at 2:30, it is hard to put the lofty-sounding traits such as courtesy, class, and humility into action.

Take, for example, the following situation: Marsha, the dynamic leader of the most profitable division in the company, has been resisting the acquisition of a wireless communication device.

> **The Wrong Move.** To continue working "the old way."
> **The Consequence.** Marsha will be harried and unproductive. She will continue to struggle with an e-mail load that keeps her tied to her desk after hours and before and after out-of-office meetings, at the expense of one-on-one or team meetings in the field.

> **The Right Move.** To take the time to acquire the device, using minutes between meetings to stay in touch and better delegate the issues that arise all day long.
> **The Consequence.** Marsha is freed to attend more business and personal events, and she can relax knowing she is staying in touch, while she controls access to her time.

It is important to focus on your responsibilities relating to the team's process and structure, plan, and people, but be aware that activities within this focus are not always readily apparent. Sometimes the work you should be doing to be best focused right now will not readily present itself on your "calendar." With those requests or communications that don't warrant your attention right now, find a way to respectfully and promptly deal with them in a manner which reinforces your reputation as just a decent person. Influential and inspirational leadership follows from your ability to energize those around you to get the desired results of a common goal, but you are also successful because people like you, have a relationship with you, and want to work for you.

SUMMING UP

Consider the following strategies for energizing your team to get results:

1. **Show up.** Get into the environment with your team on a regular basis to share information.
2. **Be available.** Let people come to you for informal guidance as much as reasonably possible. Don't make getting an appointment with you a discouraging ordeal.
3. **Have presence in your absence.** Expect people to make decisions, when they need to be made, even when you are absent. Not making a decision can be worse than making a wrong decision.
4. **Follow up.** Things can blow up, especially when you are working with inexperienced people. Help people understand what went wrong by asking the right questions: "What happened?" "Do you know you made the wrong decision?" "What have you learned?"
5. **Know when and how to acknowledge and recognize good results.** Insightful rewards and recognition often have greater personal meaning than the biweekly pay deposit. By giving your team members the freedom to make decisions, flextime when required, a gift specific to a hobby or special pleasure, the acknowledgment of day-to-day achievements, and your willingness to celebrate achievements, you will receive in return a priceless gift: loyalty. It is amazing how rare true praise is. That's why it's so valuable. To give true praise takes confidence as well as personal insight on what is important to your team and the individuals on it.

Chapter 4

GETTING RESULTS IS SIMPLE—DO WHAT MATTERS!

Real Life

It's frustrating when you don't get the results you want. There is little worse than consistent errors by a team member or the surprise of something not happening when you fully expected it to be done.

To meet your responsibilities, and the expectations of your superiors, you need to know yourself, know your team, and know what your managers require of you. Often this simply boils down to three things:

1. See the big picture, and be accountable for it.
2. Give clear directions on what is expected, and then make sure it happens.
3. Create an atmosphere of trust.

To see the big picture, you must know exactly what the expectations are of you. Make *sure* you know. Exactly where do you and your team need to be at the end of an expected time period? What are the numbers? Don't get tripped up because you didn't have the courage to probe and clarify enough with your boss. This is where who you are and how you lead really counts. Without the ability to get the right information, you will not be able to articulate a vision and mandate that commands the best from your team.

This vision and mandate must then be made absolutely clear to every team member. Your team's success depends on your deft ability to articulate accountabilities, to monitor progress, and follow up immediately on both successes and weaknesses. When people know *what* they need to achieve, *when* they need to achieve it and *how* to achieve it, you will get the results you want. The fact that they are led by an authentic and caring person who is detached enough to communicate well and make difficult decisions that keep the team on track also helps.

THE A-B-C-D MODEL OF LEADERSHIP STYLE

In our experience, four characteristics stand out as essential to get the day-to-day job of leadership done successfully. These traits can be easily remembered as The A-B-C-D Model of Leadership Style:

- **Accountable** for the Plan. Full stop.
- **Bold** and able to draw the very best from each person on the team.
- **Caring** about the success of the team and each person on it, and the stakeholders it serves.
- **Detached** enough from the team to make difficult decisions.

ACCOUNTABLE

"The Buck Stops Here" said a sign on the desk of Harry S. Truman, 33rd President of the United States. And what a reassuring phrase it is: a reflective statement of the boss's acknowledgement that, win or lose, the overall success of the team is on his or her shoulders. This acknowledgement of accountability helps to create trust and the quality of trust is at the core of any player–coach relationship.

Although there are many behaviors and activities that create or destroy trust, a key one in the coach–player relationship is the belief in the player's mind that the coach will stand behind him if he fails and, moreover, give him the proverbial second chance, with the necessary coaching and mentoring to be successful.

So what does accountability really mean and how do you practice it on a daily basis? You need to:

- Know your plan.
- Have an implemented strategy with a no-surprises, follow-up process.
- Know how to apologize well.

Know Your Plan

You can't be truly accountable unless you fully understand the benchmarks against which you and your team will be measured. For this reason, we believe that accountability begins in private, when you take the time, likely lots of time, to really understand the goals and objectives of the team. A revealing question to ask yourself is: When all is said and done, what really matters to the people who are interested in my team? Meeting the sales targets? Having clean audits? Scoring well on customer satisfaction surveys? Receiving positive publicity in the media? Your team's performance measurements will be unique to your team; for simplicity, we refer throughout the book to "the Plan," as a shorthand way of referring to whatever is essential for you and your team to achieve.

Before doing anything else, take time to reflect on your Plan and those aspects of it that will truly be considered by senior management to measure your team's success against the Plan. Sometimes the *published* key performance indicators differ significantly from the indicators that really matter, and if you lead your team to succeed against the wrong indicators, your team will obviously not be successful in the long run. Not only will the team miss it's Plan, the team members will almost certainly be defeated and discouraged, having invested significant time and energy running down the wrong path.

Have an Implemented Strategy, with a No-Surprises, Follow-Up Process

Once you are crystal clear on the "real" Plan your team has been assigned, it is most important to:

1. Understand your Plan so thoroughly that you can explain both the Plan and your implementation strategy to anyone, anytime, without the comfort blanket prop of overhead slides!
2. Develop a strategy (and implementation process) to achieve the Plan.
3. Put effective and time-sensitive processes in place so that your team and your personal leadership of it operate on a "no surprises" basis. Naturally, as leader, you are accountable for things that go wrong, *but your job is to plan to succeed, not plan to fail,* and the right processes will take you a very long way to having some degree of comfort that you will *not* end up accountable for a crash-and-burn.

Know How to Apologize Well

We come now to the implicit meaning in being fully accountable: no matter how well you understand your Plan, implement a great strategy, and stay on top of developments, at some time or other in your leadership career, you or a team member will screw up, forget something, and make a mistake. Inside the team, you have an opportunity to work with whomever made the error to find the lesson in it so that at the very least, the error has one positive outcome. But beyond the team, or if the mistake was yours alone, your team needs to see your accountability in action. Often this means both an explicit acceptance of responsibility and an apology.

Apologizing is likely the first "etiquette" we learn as children, right along with the words *please* and *thank you*, yet its use in leadership seems to have dropped off remarkably in recent years.

James Gray, a media strategist and communication skills coach, points out that "Progressive leaders in the workplace know that stonewalling is never the way to go; it has a short, unsustainable shelf life." He notes that if you truly intend to rebuild the trust that the incident has caused, an apology must be:

- Specific, referring precisely to the offending incident
- Unqualified
- Sincere and from the heart

To those who say that apologizing can be an admission of guilt or a sign of weakness detrimental to the organization, the quip, "get over yourself," comes to mind.

For one thing, most incidents requiring an apology are in no way connected to the possibility of litigation. Even where litigation is a possibility, sincerely contrite organizations and individuals may have more to gain in enhanced reputation and reduced damages by a well-planned apology than they have to lose.

More to the point, legal ramifications are not usually the issue; at issue is whether you have the confidence as a leader to step up and say, "It's my responsibility. I'm sorry. How can we make this right?" The bottom line is that apologies usually only come from the strongest and most effective leaders.

The flip side to apologizing well, is praising well. Someone once said that a good leader inspires others with confidence in him; a great leader inspires them with confidence in themselves.

HOW CAN WE MAKE THE PEOPLE AROUND US MORE CONFIDENT IN THEMSELVES?

Take the time to praise well. We know intuitively that most people respond better to praise than to criticism, but for some reason we are less generous in our praise of day-to-day accomplishments than we are with what we euphemistically call "constructive criticism," which is criticism nevertheless. The wise and effective leader provides authentic, truthful praise, that is not only complimentary and makes the person feel good, but is also like a good apology in that it is specific, unqualified, and sincere.

We often muddy praise with the word *but.* "That was a great presentation, really thorough, but next time let's makes sure the projector is working well." If it was a terrific presentation, there is a pretty good chance that the presenter is kicking *himself* about the projector! Or perhaps that "but" issue could be mentioned later in a more formal review of the presentation. The point is, nothing douses effective praise like that little word *but.*

Even the top salespeople on the team and the biggest self-promoters in the company probably have huge doubts about their abilities. The better the sales in the last quarter, the more anxious they are the next quarter! Most people underestimate their value and assess themselves in a way that is "off the mark" and even destructive: you should seek to build people up whenever possible and save your constructive criticism for your well-planned coaching sessions.

Be Bold

You may not think of yourself as *bold,* a word conjuring up other words like *forceful* and *daring,* maybe even *brash* and *flashy.* We don't mean those characteristics at all. Being bold refers to your willingness to boldly—and with purpose—coach your team members so they can be their best. This may well be the single most difficult task of a leader. Consistently and effectively being bold in focused, directed conversations is one of the hardest things for a leader to do.

Hold the Meat

Meaningful and constructive criticism can sometimes be best delivered by first describing the positive contribution of the listener, then the troubling issue at hand, and lastly (the top of the "sandwich") further reinforcement of the individual's worth to end the feedback on a positive note.

A senior manager who subscribed to the "sandwich theory" had to laugh when a colleague commented that some of the "sandwiches" the executive gave him were so heavy on the meat that they were very hard to swallow! While said in jest, the comment does point out that at times as a leader, you simply do need to come right out and say what needs to be fixed. Truthfully, some of the most direct and at times difficult conversations have resulted in the most meaningful changes. This does not make them easy, however, and we suggest that it would be the rare leader who doesn't benefit from ongoing refreshers on what effective coaching is all about.

The advances in technology and travel mean that any organization (corporate, not for profit, charitable) in any field (sports, entertainment, goods, or services) is up against worldwide competition, 24 hours a day. If your team can't produce a successful play, game, widget or service, the consuming market quickly moves on. It's that simple. And the only way that your team can survive in this global arena is to get inside the head of your players and understand how they tick. That sort of connection almost invariably requires you to confront team members when things aren't working. This allows you to explore what is really going on and how you can work with the team member to find a solution.

Be Caring

Years ago, employees at two large energy companies referred to their employers' merger as a marriage of the popular cuddly figure the Care Bear to the action figure GI Joe, with the sentiment clearly being conveyed from the top that the Care Bear stuff needed to go. We'd like to think that since then, corporate attitudes have changed but clearly there are many in leadership roles today that view "caring about employees" as a pejorative concept.

A more progressive (and successful) attitude is that a manager or coach of human beings who doesn't sincerely care about people would be smart to consider a new line of work. Like it or not, caring about the people on your team is an essential precursor to telling them the truth when the "truth" includes feedback that may be perceived as painful.

Daniel Goleman's work on emotional intelligence (EI) considers five aspects of EI, the last two of which are empathy and social skills. Empathy, the ability to relate to what another person is thinking or feeling, allows a leader to not only lead individuals but also work with them in such a way that they blend as a team. It also is the underpinning for a leader who really functions well when thrown into a new culture, whether that is a new department or a country on the other side of the world. Empathy also equips the leader to effectively coach and mentor top talent.

Social skills are equally important, giving a leader the confidence to build bridges between himself, his team, their clients, and other parts of the organization through the "idle chitchat" that comes easily to the socially skilled person. In our experience, having lunch in the office lunch room on a regular basis, engaging in whatever topic is under discussion, quickly allows the team to see the leader as a person and allows the leader to pick up on brewing problems or concerns. However, lacking a combination of empathy and social skills, a leader's visit to the lunch room could be disastrous, if she thinks, for example, that it is the time and place to hold court on the team's productivity challenges in the year ahead.

There is of course a time and place to convey the hard messages and difficult decisions, but that aspect of the leadership role is simplified for the socially skilled leader who has made the effort to really get to know the people around her, on a 360-degree basis within the organization, and outside of it.

In theory you may be agreeing that "caring" does fit within what we are referring to as the A-B-C-D characteristics of a leader. But how do you actually practice the art of caring as a leader? Here are two key points to establishing yourself as a truly caring leader:

- **Develop reciprocity.** Personal relationships develop based on reciprocity: over time, we develop a friendship or a romantic relationship as a result of the give and take of confidences, mutual interest in one another's well being, and two-way conversations. At the risk of sounding harsh, there is no assumed reciprocity promise in the leadership role. Maturity in leading people means caring about the individuals making up the team from day one, with no expectations that those individuals will care about you. Like it or not, you must earn your team's respect and trust.

On the other hand, the key to leadership success is the ability to build and sustain relationships that are based on reciprocity. When one party does all the giving and the other all the taking, there is an imbalance that will lead to failure. The successful leader brings talent together through a process of relationship building and reciprocity to move the team forward in the direction it needs to go. That requires equal give and take and the ability to draw on the leadership of the individuals on the team. The leader sets the stage for reciprocity on a task-by-task basis by driving the energy around team members and encouraging each team member to fully participate and contribute.

- **Communicate Consistently and Fully.** Nothing conveys a sense that you are genuine in your interest in and respect for the team more than effective communication, practiced daily by:

  a. **Sharing** as much information as possible. Within the appropriate constraints of confidentiality, you can make it your routine practice to share information such as management reports and your minutes from "head office" meetings. A perennial complaint from people is that they just don't know what is going on and are only given information on a need-to-know basis.

  b. **Seeking** the opinion and ideas of team members on a regular basis and letting them know that you value their experience and input. The more often you do this, the more creative the flow of information will be from your team, and the higher the level of excitement and enthusiasm generated in the team. People want to be consulted and needed!

c. **Involving your team** in decision making as much as possible.

d. **Giving people credit** for the ideas they have that turn out well.

e. **Talking up** the successes of team members to people in and beyond the team. Why not mention that the person on your team passed her chartered financial analyst exam or that the top boss really liked another person's idea for an incentive program? *Everyone loves to be connected to a winning team.* Talking up your individual and team accomplishments and celebrating them with the rest of the world just makes good business sense. Always strive to turn "I" into "we" and help your team establish pride.

f. **Connecting** every day with the people on your team and as often as you can with the people that work for or with your team members. Frequent communication with all levels of the organization will increase the frequency, quantity, and quality of the feedback you get. A senior leader who relies on the annual employee survey results or other official means of soliciting feedback will be woefully uninformed.

BE DETACHED

The more that a leader can remain detached from the rising heat and emotion in a situation, the greater her ability to stay in control and observe objectively. In turn, this allows the leader to continue to receive and really hear what is being said and of course stops the leader from blurting out equally emotive statements that can be endlessly repeated around the water cooler!

There is also another aspect of detachment that is an essential leadership trait, and that is the ability to put team success ahead of any individual's short- or medium-term interests. The obvious example is when the organization is going to part ways with an individual. Whether this severance of the relationship is due to individual performance or the simple need to reduce costs, a leader's effectiveness in both the decision and its implementation is reduced if he loses sight of the big picture. The "big picture" of any team is that:

- The leader–team member relationship should never be—in fact, cannot be—a personal one. Leadership carried out with empathy and warmth never loses its core essence as a professional relationship in which the leader's first responsibility is to the organization and the Plan.
- The inability to make the tough decision about poor performer A directly hurts strong performers B, C, and D.

Done correctly, the leader's job of terminating the relationship can be part of a process or stage that the departing individual eventually views as a positive turning point in his career. And, most importantly, such a parting can be respectful, and in many cases, the long-term relationship between the manager and parting employee can even be preserved.

KEEP MANY BALLS IN THE AIR

All great leaders have certain specific traits as they balance what at first seem to be conflicting interests: responsibility for the success of both the team and the individuals on it, all the while demonstrating an active interest in the personal well-being of the individuals beyond their participation in the team. In developing and evaluating your own style, and why it may or may not be working to get results with your direct reports and your superiors, it helps to remember the A-B-C-D Model of Leadership Style.

Checklist: Great Leadership Attributes of Today's Top Manager

□   Great sensitivity to social, technological, and demographic realities

- Ability to grasp those realities and seize opportunities at the right time
- Focus on changing the size and scope of the organization
- Courage to take risks and the perseverance to see things through
- Ability to earn trust though visionary leadership—a strong understanding of the future and how to get there
- Ability to expand the vision to and with team members in a disciplined way
- Ability to bring routine to the strategic vision by implementing a viable structure with defined processes
- Superior ability to tap into the psyche and potential of team members
- Great integrity (great leaders do the right thing for the stakeholders to a plan rather than for themselves)
- Ability to inspire people to achieve high goals and work at their personal maximum potential

SUMMING UP

Dwight D. Eisenhower once defined leadership as the art of getting someone else to do something you want done because he wants to do it. Leadership is really about the follower: if you can successfully set a stage, provoke thought, and compel each individual to give his or her personal best in meeting a common, mutually desired goal, then you can get out of the way and let the actors act, the athletes compete, and the writers produce.

In being a facilitator of great results, consider developing an arsenal of reinforcing questions to ask in guiding your team to successful and anticipated results; one that will emphasize your characteristics as an accountable, bold, caring, and detached leader. Some questions to consider asking include:

1. What's important today?
2. Are we meeting targets?

3. Why? Why not?
4. What's missing?
5. What's working?
6. How can I help you?
7. Has this meeting been helpful?

Then remember to share as much information as you can, praise well, and apologize sincerely when you make a mistake.

Do It Yourself!
Responsibility 1: Personal Leadership

- **Be authentic.** Your team knows the "real you" so work on ensuring that your influence is a positive influence on the team results. Your ability to lead and get great results depends on your credibility to your team.
- **Earn respect.** Don't use your title or position as a means to achieve goals; work toward being genuinely respected by your team for your integrity and your ability to do the things that matter to the team's success, day after day.
- **Have a healthy ego.** No matter how high up on the corporate ladder you climb, don't use excuses to get out of doing the right thing and stay rooted in your values. Remember the basics of being a good person: good manners, humility, a belief that everyone is worthy of your respect. As a leader, you are in service to others.
- **Embrace change.** Keep an eye on the big picture: are you making the best choices for this stage of your life, the team's stage, your colleagues' lives?
- **Acknowledge different choices.** Not everyone on your team will make the same life-stage choices as you; their decisions are neither right nor wrong. The question is whether the team can accommodate their choices while still achieving the team's Plan.

- **It's about relationships**. Avoid the "harried leader" syndrome. Know when to step back and take time to connect with people on an impromptu basis: most team successes occur outside of scheduled meetings and e-mails . . . notice what's going on.
- **Winners celebrate and losers check the rules**. Never forget you are completely accountable for the achievement of your team's Plan; there is no blaming anyone else when it "doesn't happen." Stand behind your team in a slump; celebrate with them in success. Influential leadership is about the followers.
- **Energize your team**. Know your team's real purpose. Understand exactly what your team needs to achieve and follow up relentlessly to make sure that it is accomplished.
- **Show courtesy, class, and humility**. Seek out what you do wrong and be humble about what you do right. Acknowledge the weaknesses in your leadership style; most of the time we know what we can be doing better. Do it.
- **Be detached**. Worry when you don't get bad news and don't get defensive when you do. In the big picture, negative feedback won't make or break you; act on it and remember that leadership is a continuous improvement process. To stay in control, really hear what is being said.

RESPONSIBILITY 2

THE TEAM STRUCTURE

"Lower level people manage things. Middle managers manage people. Senior managers manage processes . . . while middle managers are concerned about logistics, scheduling and relationships."

Michel Robert,
Product Innovation Strategy

Real Life

As we discussed in Responsibility 1, as the leader, you have a huge influence over your team members and thus the team's success. But even the best leader is still only one person. With today's enormous communication demands and fast pace, one person is incapable of achieving the team's goals.

Over the past decade, leadership courses at all levels have incorporated concepts such as relationship management, team goal setting, and team effectiveness along with interpersonal skills such as resolving workplace conflict. In short, leadership today and plan management is all about the effectiveness of the team.

For your team to do what it needs to do, your challenge is to assess the structure in which you lead and the types of processes you have in place. This is critical if your company's increasing productivity requirements are to be met, year after year.

> The personal opportunity for you is that if you are able to take a group of people and make them better as a team than as individuals, the world is your oyster and there is nothing you can't do as a leader.

Responsibility 2—the team structure—suggests some ways to achieve the collaboration that is so essential today for team success and individual accomplishment. Turning a group of individuals into a team requires you to:

- Hire the best possible people to meet team goals.
- Engage team members so effectively that you get the best of their strengths and the least of their weaknesses, working harmoniously as a group.
- Help your team members become self-motivated individuals: challenged and fulfilled over the long term.

The only way to succeed in these objectives is through a structure that considers all of the relevant internal and external influences and obstacles for your team and allows every team member to feel involved and important. To begin, here are two key ideas:

- **Top Dogs Be Gone:** Gone are the days when a leader could simply talk with the senior team, ignore everyone else, and make all the big decisions on his own. Today, that type of management will quickly lead to disinterested and disengaged team members, anxiously seeking employment elsewhere.
- **Mentors and Role Models Step Up:** People will follow your lead, doing what you do, not what you say *they* should do. Accordingly, a structure or process that you personally aren't immersed in will quickly lose its vitality and impact. You've got to talk the talk and walk the walk with your people.

Let's turn now to creating the ideal environment for your team.

Chapter 5

THE TEAM AROUND
YOUR TEAM

Real Life

Here's the challenge: meeting ever-increasing productivity targets in today's rapidly changing, highly competitive business environment. You know that viewing yourself simply as the leader of your team is not going to cut it if your team is to succeed against the competition. You and your team have to do more and know more than in the past.

This begins with an understanding of all the stakeholders relying on your team's efforts. This includes not only your clients, but also the company's other employees, suppliers, the shareholders, the families of your team members, and everyone in the community, including your competitors. The needs and influence of these constituents must shape every move. Your awareness of the impact of your team's actions on all of the stakeholders will help you rethink your operating structure, as well as your leadership style in managing it. This is critical if your company's increasing productivity targets are to be met year after year, often without the benefit of increasing resources.

WHO CARES ABOUT WHAT YOUR TEAM ACHIEVES?

Everyone. We often overlook some of the interested parties; for example, each team member's circle of family and friends is connected to our team and yet, within a corporate environment, we often only think of spouses or partners at the holiday party when they are thanked for their support. Managers can and should do better than this.

Consider, for example, the following situation: During a natural disaster, a hotel employee worked throughout one night, trying to stop the flooding in his home's basement. The next morning, he called into work asking for the day off. He was given the time, and in addition his boss sent two hotel employees with plumbing experience and a meal from the hotel kitchen to the employee's house.

The result? The manager's acts of kindness (which were within the hotel's policies to carry out) conveyed to the employee a sense of caring about him as a person in a far more meaningful way than a team retreat or bonding exercise.

Similarly, our clients, other partners in the enterprise, suppliers, shareholders, senior management and owners, the public, industry associations . . . each of these have an interest in our team's success or failure and yet we tend to not consider them unless confronted with a specific need or request. Take these stakeholders into account in developing your team structure. You need their support; in fact, it is absolutely critical to your team's success.

Stakeholder interconnectivity and its effect on your team can be illustrated in another way. Some of you may remember puzzle rings from your childhood. A puzzle ring was a series of interconnected rings, four or five of them, that fit together neatly on your finger. When you took it off, the rings fell into a slinkylike structure; each ring clearly visible yet intertwined with each other ring in the group. Thinking of the parties who affect and are affected by your team in this way may highlight our point. Considering the interests of the team's "partners" before they have a chance to seek us or our team out with a problem or demand, allows better engagement of the team members in not only what the team is expected to do, but the team's overall goals.

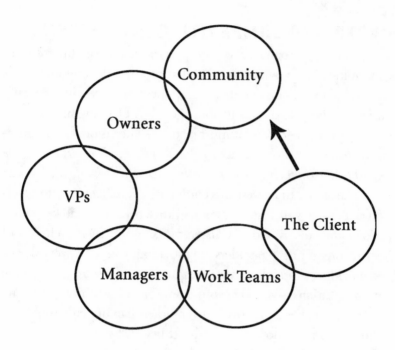

A potent example of the interaction between company employees and the rest of the world is the blog phenomenon. Business-Week Online had a frank talk with its readers in May 2005, when it defined blogs as "simply the most explosive outbreak in the information world since the Internet itself... [declaring blogs to be] not a business elective... [but] a prerequisite." At that time there were approximately nine million blogs, with an estimated 40,000 new ones arriving every day.

Astute leaders know that surpassing the competition depends on the degree to which the team embraces opportunities to reach out to the individual and intertwined rings on their puzzle ring. To do so, new leaders can more successfully involve their teams by continually asking questions such as:

- Why do we do the things we do and for whom?
- Who can have an impact on our success?
- How are we involving them in what we do?

CAPTURING COMPETITIVE INTELLIGENCE

The professional manager who designs the right structure for team communication provides the glue that captures the ongoing needs of stakeholders. This is a critical component of success in managing businesses today, and is really nonnegotiable. Devising such a structure is part of the job and it must be done. The visionary and innovative leader, however, has a broader mandate. *He or she knows the importance of capturing and integrating such feedback into the business plan.* The ability to harvest this competitive intelligence with precision can propel you past your competitors, because it will keep your team highly motivated. By listening carefully to the clues and instructions your stakeholders are providing you with every day— and providing a formal process for capturing and disseminating these communications—you give your team the opportunity to nail the needs of your clients and overdeliver rather than underdeliver.

So how do you do that, exactly? It begins by creating an environment in which team members have ample opportunity to interact with all internal and external stakeholders and thereby assume even informal leadership roles. These communications can be most effectively used when the leader provides structure.

STRUCTURED COMMUNICATIONS STRATEGIES

You know you are doing things well when your customers seek you out. Are you capturing these opportunities? Consider the following ideas:

- **Prospect management and stakeholder identification screens:** Every new name is captured in a prospect management system that sorts the stakeholders into categories and channels follow-up communications by profile to the right department, for example, by: (1) Prospective clients by product, (2) prospective employees, (3) prospective suppliers, and (4) prospective shareholders.
- **Make it feel like home:** Someone must be in charge of following up with these prospective stakeholders by e-mail,

mail, and phone. Every opportunity to "touch" a prospect with human care is a step forward in building a committed and reciprocal relationship. Let prospects know that when they care enough to come into contact with your team, your team cares enough to respond in a meaningful way.

- **How can we help you?** Make that the first question, front and center with every communication. Before you provide your laundry list of stellar features of your particular product or service, you have to know and understand the needs of your clients—and the only way to find out what these needs are is to ask and then *listen*. Why are people interested in your product? What caused them to come to your environment? What will compel them to stay and buy? Or stay as a team member? Capture their needs as you listen; then add them meticulously and steadfastly to the list of needs and desired benefits mentioned by others. This provides you with the benefits you'll want to market and the competitive intelligence you need to lead in your marketplace.
- **Here's why you should deal with us:** Taking the clues from the needs of your prospects and your existing customers, describe why you are so confident that your team can meet your stakeholders' needs. Create a benefit list that covers not just the features of the particular product, service, or environment you provide, but also the benefits of the relationship with your firm and its team.
- **Make it edgy and make it happen.** Your prospect and client interface structure, whatever form it takes, must be consistent. *Demand accountability: to make great things happen, the team needs to buy into the notion that formal procedures, deadlines, and progress reports transform intentions into reality.*

ENGAGE EVERY SEGMENT

Your ability to engage team members with stakeholders inside and outside the organization is particularly important if you lead people born after 1975. People in that demographic segment often feel

unfamiliar in a traditional corporate hierarchy with top-down decision making. Working and playing hard, they struggle to feel valuable in roles in large anonymous organizations. They see these roles
as unimportant and narrow. Despite the fact that some are loners,
they are accustomed to having the ability to communicate constantly with literally the entire world. In fact, they are extremely
good at this: early adopters of communication methods and new
technology of all kinds, they know how to be informed. As their
manager, it is essential that you appreciate their capabilities and
find ways to integrate them on the job. Beyond encouraging them
to use their communication skills in their roles on the team, it is
your interest in developing relationships with them and encouraging them to do the same that will pay off with the post-1975 group.

WHEN "THEY JUST DON'T GET IT!"

Think hard about how to connect and maximize relationships with
generations later than your own: they represent your team's future
success and likely much of its current possibilities. Every time you
find yourself rolling your eyes and saying, "They just don't get it!"
ask yourself what *you* aren't getting. A recent Youthography survey,
conducted by *The Globe and Mail*, of 1,200 employed Canadians
under age 30 stated that more than 80 percent planned to be "outta
here" within two years. The survey noted that younger workers are
quickly bored in situations where information is disseminated
downwards on a need-to-know basis, especially if they sense
that they have little impact on decisions. If nothing they think
or believe really matters, it is just a job to them, not a relationship.
You need to figure out what matters to the younger people on
your team and how to lead them in a directed way. Take advantage
of their incredible natural potential for community building—
within your team, the wider organization, and your marketplace.
Include them.

The Youthography study also looked at job commitment. Many
younger people do not view career stability in the same positive
way that previous generations did, intent on receiving the five

weeks of holidays and gold watch after 25 years with the company. Accordingly, those born after 1975 are quick to seek a role elsewhere when their current job is not fulfilling their expectations. The question is, how do you keep them engaged? The Youthography survey ranked their top priorities at work as follows:

62.5%: Interesting work
61%: Compensation
49.5%: Job flexibility
43%: Work environment

The survey provides some clues in structuring environments for younger workers: make sure you give them interesting work, adequate compensation for their lifestyle which can include time off (many of them have difficulty with the concept of five-day work weeks and the whole nine-to-five routine) and a collaborative environment in which they can *learn to be leaders, have an impact, and earn respect.*

CREATE INDIVIDUAL AND TEAM OWNERSHIP OPPORTUNITIES

It isn't just those in their twenties and thirties who seek greater meaning to their work. All employees are increasingly seeking the opportunity to be part of the action and have a say in what goes on in the workplace. *People like to get involved!* Even senior management recognizes this phenomenon. In the 2005 Canadian Corporate Culture Study conducted by Waterstone Human Capital, senior management at 107 companies were asked what Canadian corporate cultures they admired. Top of the list? WestJet Airlines Ltd. which has as its hallmark the active participation of employees in the company.

What was the corporate structure and process that allowed the entire team of stakeholders to be pointed in the same direction? WestJet accomplished team success through profit sharing, share participation, and a raft of mechanisms to ensure employee input is obtained. It is also interesting to note that at WestJet, employees are referred to as "people" and "owners"; customers are referred to as "guests"! In fact the ownership concept has been the subject of WestJet's billboards and successful television messaging.

In the United States, Genentech, a major biotech company with estimated revenues of 6.6 billion dollars, topped *Fortune* magazine's 2006 list of The 100 Best Companies to Work For. The key to Genentech's success—and its true competitive advantage—lies in its corporate culture. Instead of allowing market data and return-on-investment analysis to drive research initiatives, the company concentrates on developing "drugs that really matter"—a corporate philosophy that instills pride and commitment in Genentech employees. In addition to onsite daycare, generous stock options, and numerous other personal perks, the company encourages scientists and engineers to spend 20 percent of their time working on their own pet projects, awards sabbaticals to prevent burnout, and celebrates employee contributions to business achievements.

In short, the culture that you develop with your team is in your control and of utmost importance to your team's ability and capacity to handle increasing demands from internal and external stakeholders. Be creative about this. Listen with purpose to find out exactly what it takes to engage people on your team. Ask questions like:

- What did you accomplish today?
- What worked really well for you today?
- What would you do differently next time?
- What should *we* do differently?

Some Personal Insights on Employee Engagement

Think about it. It's so much easier to participate when you know that what you think about and what you do matters. Asking your employees their opinion is a powerful path to engagement. Going one step further, that is, capturing their best thoughts and implementing them into the team plan, provides not only the ultimate compliment, but is an innovative strategy for succession planning. Giving your team members an opportunity to participate in a genuine way demonstrates your personal commitment to top talent development.

ASSIST WITH TIME MANAGEMENT

Time matters, and careful management is essential to your team's operating structure. As we discussed in Responsibility 1, you first need to manage your own time well so that you can properly perform the most important aspects of your job. But beyond that personal time management, you also must find a way for the team to do what needs to be done without expecting or asking people to sacrifice their personal time or health. Work hard at building an operating structure that fits with your team's whole lives.

A key component of an effective operating structure is that certain deadlines and requirements are nonnegotiable. No one on your team should be compensating for another team member's failure to deliver. A missing or ineffective cog in the wheel means that you have dropped the ball as the leader and your action is required. Be clear that the team's success depends on each person pulling his or her weight and working hard to ensure that jobs are done well and on time. Carelessness, lack of attention, or other attributes of poor performance have no place in a fast-paced, streamlined, team environment, and addressing these issues is your number one job.

EMPOWER KNOWLEDGE LEADERS

A great way to engage everyone on the team is to look for opportunities to encourage people to be informal leaders. Strong team members who are willing to teach, mentor, and coach others on the team provide you with key influencers across the team. Your role as the leader of course then becomes more collaborative, and you have also found a way to encourage high achievers in the group to step up to the plate and show what they can do in leadership situations. Providing these opportunities to develop can make all the difference to high achievers who are looking to move up in the organization but are not yet ready for a formal promotion.

SUMMING UP

Do you need to reshape your role in leading your team? Can you lead in a more open and collaborative way than you may currently be doing in a traditional organizational structure? What new or revised structure or process is required to enable greater communication among management, all team members, and the *field of play*—the environment in which we serve our clients? The transition of your workplace into a more collaborative team will allow you to clear your slate of daily minutiae and become more effective yourself. Consider your role in the following objectives of collaborative leadership:

- Focusing on implementing the company's strategic goals in the context of the "field of play."
- Enabling change and collaboration that results in innovative execution by your team members.
- Expanding opportunities for communications with all stakeholders—internal and external.
- Making it easy for prospective new stakeholders—clients, employees, suppliers, shareholders, board members—to feel the buzz and excitement about your team.
- Managing the work your employees do, day by day, week by week, ensuring that everyone is on plan.

It is critical for you and the team to consider the world beyond the team's own members. No matter what responsibilities a particular team has, the many "interested parties" who can provide feedback from outside the team, are the eyes and ears to future success.

Chapter 6

COMMUNICATE: EVERYONE INTO THE POOL!

Real Life

As you review your current operating structure, one of the first considerations needs to be the way in which you and your team communicate to the outside.

In many companies the internal hurdles make interaction with the outside—where the company really needs to compete and win—virtually impossible. But as the leader, you must control what you and your team do, and when and how you do it, by deciding which demands will be met and in what order.

A starting point if you lead a customer-focused team is to separate the activities on the field of play, the contact with the external marketplace, with those of the go team, the internal work team.

STRUCTURE TO SERVE YOUR CLIENTS AND YOUR TEAM

The level of your management position today does not preclude your managing your team with vision and with a structure that is forward thinking and innovative. In fact, so-called middle management is the perfect place for maximum impact in terms of incubating new ways to manage new challenges—both with your team and with those who will recruit you upwards. Remember, you are in charge of execution. Your team is watching you, and so are all the other stakeholders we've mentioned; a prime opportunity awaits you as an increasing number of senior executives recognize that changes in their corporate culture, and structures, are vitally needed.

A stunning 72 percent of the senior executives surveyed in the 2005 Corporate Culture Study, mentioned in Chapter 5, said that their organizations' culture is not what they desire in the future. It is important, therefore, not to shrink away from the opportunity to structure your team's operating environment with vision, even though this may not be a stated requirement of your current role. Bureaucratic clutter, internal power struggles, and office politics can cloud the real demands that effective leaders must address:

- Shareholders demand a better return for their investment every year
- Clients demand enhanced service, product improvements, choice, and value pricing
- Employees demand more meaningful work, generous time, and compensation packages
- Family and community demand their employees share their time and abilities beyond the workplace
- Individuals pressed to make more time and money demand straight-line solutions that promote and sustain mental and physical health during execution of the team's business objectives.

To lead a team with an appropriately high level of focus on what customers want and need, think about your team's activities as those which are externally focused (the field of play) and those which are the bailiwick of the internal work team, the "go team."

If your business is running a football club, for example the go team includes people involved in accounting, ticket sales, the

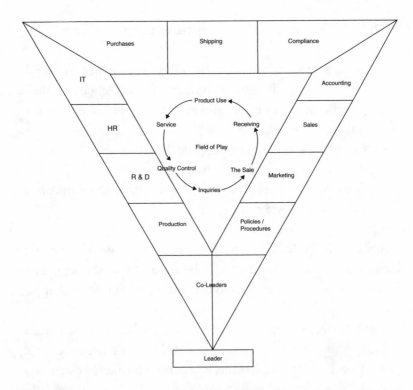

Web site, promotions, player's contracts, security, concessions, operations, and so on. This team forms a layer of activity around the team on the field of play. It may be useful to think of this concept visually, which in some organizations is called the *V-Team*, as illustrated in the diagram.

A V-Team structure requires individuals to be present around the table in their unique and important roles, to report on the activities in and around the field of play. Such a structure is easy to integrate into any existing management team and forces the team to think about what their purpose really is: the attainment of goals which can only be delivered by a concerted effort focused on the field of play. It allows you to ask direct questions such as:

- What is happening on the field of play?
- What are the customers and others on the field of play demanding?
- What do the team members working there need?

The V-Team structure has many benefits, among them:

- Team members focus on the client experience; it enables those who are in direct contact with the client to find a straight line to solution providers on the management team and company resources.
- The team aligns on common goals, rather than on the guys in sales versus those in accounting.
- The team is equipped to see who should take responsibility for what, and when.

In short, while the V-Team flattens the traditional hierarchical team structure, it also allows you to be a team-focused leader, rather than a reactive or proactive solo act, and provide informal opportunities for leadership.

The V-Team concept has been successfully used in the Pan Am and Olympic Games as a decision-making structure specifically geared to volunteer venue teams where it is considered essential to maximize the information disseminated to all volunteers regardless of their specific role. One can ask why this level of individual involvement has not been considered as essential in for-profit companies intended to operate on a permanent basis. The power of the V-Team concept is its ability to provide your team with a communication framework that includes management, customers, and people in every role: everyone working in either internal or external roles is present at the table. It is an effective way for you to:

- **Engage your team** in an environment in which each individual has the opportunity to gain new experiences through informal leadership opportunities created by the formalized team interaction. That's motivating and energizing for everyone.
- **Create a structure** where individual accountability is required to make the system work: it will soon become apparent who is pulling their weight and who is not. Rather than being accountable to you, each individual is accountable to every other member of the team, putting many of the fires that may otherwise

be on your desk back where they belong—on the desks of those who are not carrying out their responsibilities to the team.

- **Remove the bottlenecks of information.** As the leader, it is easy to get caught in the trap of being the sole information receiver, reviewer, and distributor. The V-Team structure creates a number of appropriate "touch points" for communication between the team members and internal and external stakeholders.
- **Shift your time** away from logistics, scheduling, and internal people issues to providing strategic insight critical to the success of the team.
- **Increase your own job satisfaction** by making everyone's opinion count: you will have given everyone a voice and an opportunity to influence the strategic direction of the team.

ACCOUNTABLE COMMUNICATIONS

In practice, engaging people to be accountable in a V-Team structure is simple: each team member has a formal role at regular weekly team meetings, reporting on last week's action items and discussing customer issues that arose. New action items are set for the week ahead. No team member is more important than the next in deciding on the results the team needs to achieve, and each individual's role in obtaining these results. Your role as the leader is to guide and reinforce the decisions that arise out of this process, rather than micromanaging the discussion or planning the process yourself. You will need to lead the team to consider:

- Who do we need on the team and what are their specific roles?
- How does each person on the team interact, overlap, and fit in with the other roles on the team?
- What are the skills required to achieve the required results and minimize distraction?
- What are the key operating values for each role on the team?
- How can we help the people who are not in direct contact with the customer to fully understand the client needs?

- How do we ensure we do not become a "bureaucracy"?
- How can we ensure that the team members serving customers, shareholders, and the community are getting the systems, supports, and tools required to provide outstanding service?

ON INTRODUCING INVESTIGATIVE REPORTING

In every business, the needs of the customer or client come first. Full stop. This understanding by all the members of your team will allow you to frame the consequence of "fires" as they pop up in relation to their relative importance. Each member of your team should be enlightened in the art of investigative reporting. Probe and discover, by asking simple questions: who, what, when, why, and how? For example:

1. What happened?
2. Why did it happen?
3. Who is affected?
4. When will it be corrected?
5. How does it affect our planned results?

This is an excellent exercise around the V-Team. In answering those five simple questions your team can solve problems in and around the field of play and develop processes that lead to solutions and most importantly, the avoidance of the same kind of problem in the future.

In fact, you will be surprised at the innovative ideas that will come forward from such an approach. Much more effective than a suggestion box, the flow of ideas around the V-Team and into and out of the field of play is the first step in creating an environment responsive to the external stakeholders. Call it what you like, but we all know that labels such as "highly attentive client service" lead directly to the very best source of new business: referrals from satisfied customers. And in today's influential blog environment, concepts like word-of-mouth referrals have immensely powerful impact to millions of potential new customers.

ENABLING VIRTUAL BRAINSTORMING

Imagine continuous brainstorming for product improvement and enhancement not only with your V-Team but with your customers too! If the nature of your business allows you to do so, provide a structure around which these community dialogues can evolve. By doing this, your team is conducting continuous customer research surveys with the benefit of reacting immediately to your customer's feedback.

ADDRESSING COMMUNICATION OVERLOAD AND BUILDING COMMUNITY

The V-Team approach, with its emphasis on linking team members with either an internal or external focus, can also help your team address, harness, and capture effectively the overwhelming number of communications it receives every day, and in fact, provide the capacity to effectively handle more.

The onslaught of communications into companies is considered to be a problem in many organizations and yet it is primarily through this communication that your team can learn more about your marketplace, your customers, and your potential employees. In short, the more adept your team is at tapping into this information, the more likely you are to catapult ahead of the competition ... and meet or exceed your plan.

Some Personal Insights: On Distracting E-Mails

A leader's job is to guide the activity around all of the communications received by the team. Rather than banning e-mail, as some leaders have done, recognize the pitfall of continuing random communication as distracting and exhausting for team members constantly forced into react mode. Demand that team members think about an accountable and measureable approach to communications.

In order to capture the constant communications from the external stakeholders in a meaningful way, you will need to sort and channel them purposefully. If you can do that successfully your random communications will turn into highly confidential and influential competitive intelligence which your company can then use to beat the direct competition.

MAKE IT YOUR PRIORITY TO CREATE POLICIES AND PROCEDURES

Begin as a team to discuss the nature of continuous in- and outbound communication and its impact on various stakeholders—the team, the organization, the client, and the community—and how to handle it most effectively. Then define the process for capturing internal and external communications on a regular basis. You will also want a process for recording these daily information bites into the policies and procedures of the company—the street smarts—literally as they happen. These in effect are the how-to instructions and action templates which enable the team's essential processes. These instructions form training manuals and procedural archives that are a critical piece of corporate succession planning, which is difficult in an electronic environment.

SUMMING UP

Challenge your team to seek out, welcome, and effectively use information and feedback, from internally within your organization as well as from the external marketplace. Consider these ideas to get your team thinking in the right way:

- **Make feedback a priority on the inside.** Your priorities become your team's priorities. Let them see that you consider outside communication, especially from customers, as essential information. Encourage the team to find ways to capture this information on effective client and prospect management systems that can be sorted by your sales, marketing, administrative, and production divisions. Consider the benefits of a communications manager.
- **Capture the intelligence.** Develop an intake process for receiving, handling, interpreting, and reacting to communications received by your team.
- **Facilitate communication with communities on the outside.** Encourage clients to interact with the firm *more* often. Make it easy for them to fill in brief client surveys (three questions in an e-mail or restaurant table card). Use all of your available methods of communication to help your clients reach you 24/7, in a focused fashion. When you take control of how they communicate with you, you'll be better able to cope with and capture the communications.
- **Make it easy for clients to find you.** Encourage prospective clients to interact with your firm. Send them a sneak preview or free sample, and ask for their input and ideas. *Get them involved.* Depending on the nature of your business, investigate the many ways in which you and your team can ask for referrals from your satisfied clients. *The easiest way to do this is by exceeding people's expectations.*
- **Improve paths.** Continually work with the team and your technology to find new and better ways to interact with clients, and potential clients, in a variety of mediums. Use the V Team meetings as forums for these discussions.
- **Integrate the knowledge.** Develop a way to take the "street smarts" from the outside world and understand if and how they should be integrated into your internal policies and procedures, and operational or strategic plans. For example,

if you have created a corporate chat room, it needs to be monitored for "intelligence." Every contact must result in a full contact listing in company databases and may be enhanced with a follow-up call or e-mail.

Chapter 7

SHARE THE RISK: WHICH LEADER KNOWS BEST?

Real Life

At the root of every team's culture is how decisions are made. In a team, decision making occurs every day on issues that range from the strategic direction of the team all the way down to who gets time off. As a leader, it is your job to be aware of the ongoing decision-making process and ensure that it supports the team's success.

Individual productivity boils down to personal choice. What your team produces and achieves depends on how each team member spends his or her time: how they decide what to do, for whom, and when. It is your job as team leader to help individuals on your team understand the top priorities and encourage and enable people to make intelligent choices.

Team decision making is the next important consideration in maximizing productivity. How you make decisions—whether you make them all on your own or with the team's participation—is a significant factor in achieving an open, honest environment.

The right approach to decision making goes a long way to encouraging people to speak their minds openly and results in a high degree of buy-in to the team's direction.

INDIVIDUAL DECISION MAKING

Consider for a moment the typically high productivity of an individual in the week before a vacation. Why do we tend to get so much done at these times? Do the e-mails stop? Do the crises cease? Do even the normal challenges of every day disappear during that last week before we go on the cruise? No, of course not. We simply choose to do what's most important in the limited time we have, to get the specific results we want and need. Wouldn't it be wonderful to work with that kind of focus every day? In fact, when properly coached, people can. One way to help team members struggling with focus and priorities is to ask them to think about the demands on their plate with the benefit of some big-picture perspective. Here are some questions to engage people in setting priorities:

1. What is most important thing to do and to whom?
2. Who are the people you need to serve first?
3. When do they need to be served?
4. If fires are burning, whose fires are they to put out?
5. If you had the time to go the extra mile, what would you do?

THE MASTER OF THE MOMENT

When you and your team members all understand "the master" of the moment—the team's essential priorities—then decisions about who can do what and when become much clearer. For example, is it appropriate to place the needs of the family first when you are at work? The right answer usually is: only if there is an emergency. There is an assumption that child or elder care is in place as a prerequisite of working in the company. Outside of emergency or other highly unusual situations, questions about work-family balance need to be discussed within the parameters of the team's needs. While we have discussed the importance of a leader's empathy about life-stage challenges, devising successful solutions for ongoing family care issues is the employee's responsibility, not yours. The team's overall success against its goals is ultimately paramount.

To use another example: how much time should a team member devote to a particular charity? Looking back to the I-Chart, one might consider before taking on such an assignment that it is only possible when work and family are in balance, and if it is appropriate in relation to the self-improvement or networking opportunity provided by the charity work. In other words, taking on another activity should not interfere with existing commitments to work or family life.

'Work-life balance' must be put into perspective by every leader. With the productivity challenges faced in all workplaces, the reality is that work-life balance will be difficult, particularly for people with high career expectations. However, as stated by Michael Stern, president and CEO of Michael Stern Associates, "If you want to be on the fast track, you must recognize finding balance is your problem, not your employer's. Climbing the corporate ladder is still a 50- or 60-hour-a-week responsibility. But it doesn't have to take 90 or 100 hours ... people determined to have a life as well as a career can achieve work-life balance by being realistic, determined, and disciplined."

While accepting the 2003 International Distinguished Entrepreneur Award from the I. H. Asper School of Business, Heather Reisman, also put it well: "the reality is you can do it all—just not all at once!"

It is surprising how difficult these choices can be for some people, and you may find that it is quite simply because they do not have a framework for thinking about their priorities. Your job is to convey what really matters, without allowing your team to put every fire on your desk. Assist team members to go through decision-making processes on their own, without needing to repeatedly ask you for permission. What needs to be done? Will it get done if you do this? These are the types of questions that fully engaged team members need to ask themselves.

TEAM DECISION MAKING

Team members who are regularly involved in significant planning and decision-making activities are far more likely to work with conviction and purpose toward the successful achievement of the plans and decisions. The best solution is to help people take responsibility for more of the decisions surrounding implementation and execution of their own roles and also to have them participate in overall team decision making. This approach will free you up to think more strategically and have the time to do the parts of your job that only you can do.

> ### Some Personal Insights: On Hiring to Your Weaknesses
>
> One of the biggest mistakes you can make as a leader is not to seek your team's participation in making decisions. If you have assembled your team wisely, there will be more than one person on it who is smarter than you are. In fact, maybe they are all more talented than you, particularly in their areas of expertise. This is a great thing! Use their talents and experience by involving them as much as possible in decision making. Nevertheless as the leader you are responsible for making tough decisions that may not always be popular or obvious in the short term so it is unreasonable to suggest that you create a democracy.

Take, for example, the following scenario:

> The promotional brochures at the heart of the current marketing campaign have a significant error that will affect revenue because the pricing is wrong. There is no time to reprint them if you want to get customer response within our deadline dates.

The Wrong Move. Make the necessary phone calls either to correct or explain the error.

The Consequence. You'll be bearing the consequence of every mistake your team members make. Screwing up will be okay because you can save the day.

The Right Move. Probe. Ask what, when, why, where, and how questions. Ask for a layout of possible solutions. Get the team to tell you what the financial consequences are and how the solutions provided will address these. Then demand that the team correct the problem and meet the deadlines.

The Consequence. The mistakes will not be repeated.

Including people in decision making is not the same as seeking consensus on every decision. Leaders who do this either lack confidence or have a deep desire to be "liked" by everyone on the team. A team run by consensus becomes overloaded in making routine or obvious decisions. Time wasted on deliberating these types of decisions irritates the best people on the team, and it clouds the team's perspective on the important stuff.

Another example to consider is:

The sponsorship criteria outlined for the company's upcoming international conference clearly follows the rules set up by regulators to the industry but a minor bending of these rules would clinch a very large sponsor to come on board.

The Wrong Move. Spend time deliberating this problem.
The Consequence. A circular discussion which would lead to the same conclusion.

The Right Move. Have the employee who is asking for a decision double-check the rule book, find the rule under which this situation will be governed, clarify how the rule applies to the current situation, and then act accordingly. This action must be reported in proper fashion, together with its reasons before the leader gets involved.
The Consequence. Your employees will know that your door is open but that you will guide only when problems are presented with their potential solutions.

Factors in Deciding Who Makes Decisions

- The type of organization your team is in (small business versus large corporation)
- The type of decision (strategic versus implementation focused)
- The seniority of your team members
- Those people who have relevant information to contribute
- The degree of team or stakeholder acceptance required in order to effectively implement the decision
- The level of creativity needed to make a high quality decision
- The available time in which to make a decision

Times When You Need to Be in Control and Show Leadership

- When team members go off plan
- When there is a disagreement about moving forward with essential plans
- In certain client maintenance situations
- In times of great sorrow or great celebration
- Whenever the future success and viability of the team is concerned
- When the past comes back to haunt the team
- When there are individual or team disputes
- When your company is undergoing a merger, acquisition, or other major change
- When an employee must be hired or fired

□ When there is fraud or misrepresentation or any other substantive compliance issue

□ Where company policies and procedures are being significantly altered

MEETING ANARCHY

Whatever process you implement for decision making, it will likely result in regularly scheduled meetings. The V-Team structure we have discussed can easily facilitate such group decision making, and this structure will help you avoid "meeting anarchy"—a common syndrome in which team members spend more time planning, scheduling, canceling, and rescheduling meetings than actually getting the job done. This is completely purposeless and unproductive. With a V-Team structure in place, the meetings are prebooked in the same time slot for weeks in advance, and every person comes with a purpose and takes away a list of responsibilities for the coming week, thereby defining the agenda for next week's team meeting.

This approach eliminates any excuses by those who "didn't know" or "forgot." Those responses are not acceptable. It also puts personal-balance issues in perspective. Everyone understands that children may need to be picked up or that doctor's appointments can be inflexible. But, in principle, when everyone agrees well in advance on the regularly scheduled V-Team meeting date, unless there is an emergency or a team member is required to be out of town, attendance is mandatory.

In fact, being there and on time must be mandatory. Some offices successfully implement a "late charge" for when people don't leave in time to miss traffic or decide to pick up one last phone call before the scheduled meeting. When there is a consequence for disrespectful behaviors relating to wasting other people's time, there tends to be less of the offending behavior. Remember that an agenda with people assigned to lead the discussion on each item is essential. As well, it is good to keep the tone and energy of the meeting relaxed and open to a few laughs. This type of meeting atmosphere, which has a purpose yet is congenial, facilitates professional yet open dialogue that is solutions-oriented. You want to create a meeting culture that is akin to a think tank—thought-provoking and results oriented.

Some Personal Insights on the Use of Inner Cabinets

In many work environments, leaders face the temptation of "hidden meetings"—those conversations and discussions apart from the meetings earmarked for input from your team. Hidden meetings can arise when, human nature being what it is, higher-ups develop a couple of favorites on the team, whose opinion is greatly respected and often sought out. Over time, their advice and guidance is asked for on a wide range of matters which more properly would be placed on the agenda of the appropriate meeting.

One way of looking at "inner cabinets" is to just accept them. Accept that there are some people whose views are especially critical to the team's direction and formally set up an advisory council or executive committee that everyone knows about and has the ability to join. Done properly, this approach promotes personal growth and productivity, and important personal relationships, mutual respect and information sharing can be fostered. Those who are not in this inner cabinet must know exactly when and how they will be asked to join.

In using an inner-cabinet approach to your decision making, depending on your outlook and use of the relationship, there can be some pitfalls to watch out for:

- **Narrow focus.** Don't be too exclusive. There are lots of times when you should have the full team's input; if a significant matter was debated fully and openly with all of the team present, it may be that the ideas and arguments of the inner circle would be refuted.

- **Compromised neutrality.** Leaders need to be able to make tough decisions, even as they concern their most trusted confidants. Don't allow close personal relationships with those who are on the advisory council to affect your clear thinking.
- **Distrust.** If you are not completely open about how people get a seat at the inner cabinet, you will jeopardize your reputation as a leader who does what he says and says what he does, to everyone, all the time. Dealing differently with different team members is similar to delivering different (usually more palatable) messages to different audiences: it weakens credibility and trustworthiness in the circle where it matters most—your direct team.
- **Influence.** It takes a strong, clear-thinking leader not to be unduly influenced in the wrong direction or counter to the interest of other team members, by a self-serving inner cabinet. See through this and ensure that structure and process catch any weakness you may have in that direction.

RESPONSIBILITY FOR THE WORK

One last point concerning team decision making is the need to assign responsibility for carrying out the tasks. Doing so sets up a process resulting in immediately recognizable gaps in performance. In contrast, if no one is made clearly accountable for each step following a decision, a very real possibility is that *nothing* gets done and you will be in the position of needing to determine who was supposed to do what. This is nonproductive. Unproductive behaviors such as procrastination, inertia, and missing deadlines can be managed and changed by implementing formal project-planning procedures.

Productive change will come by showing individuals how they can achieve their goals without last-minute chaos or getting in the way of anyone else. Provide a process for doing so. You must also have expectations that the process will be adapted and followed, in the absence of a better way. Use strategic questioning.

Here's an example:

Mary is a new account executive, about to take her first sales presentation trip. Despite being provided with a list of presentation tools and materials to take with her the day before the trip, Mary's manager finds she is unprepared for the trip.

The Wrong Move. Gather and prepare the presentation, sales kits, and supplies for her.

The Consequence. You are responsible, she is not.

The Right Move. Ask a series of questions:

1. How are you going to demonstrate our product line, explain the price variations and help your clients come to the right decision?
2. How will people identify you without your name tag and business cards?
3. Was there a problem in getting the supplies?
4. Did you receive your travel itinerary and agenda?
5. Did you take the steps required to get them on a timely basis?
6. What are your options for your next trip?
7. What format of reporting will you be using to share information with the team?
8. Do you expect to get the results you want? Why or Why not?

The Consequence. Asking questions is a more influential method of communicating than telling or lecturing; parents or teachers may agree. When people don't get the results they want, avoid asking "why" questions. This will only open the door to excuses—which is a way for the person to take your focus off the issues, avoid responsibility, and justify lack of action. Ask "How" questions—how did this happen? How will this be corrected? Remember that when a discussion about an issue of responsibility results in a judgment by you (no matter how obvious the judgment is!), it will be less effective than if you provide leading questions that result in self-judgment.

Here's another example to consider:

A series of resource-wasting errors are coming from the desk of one individual, who despite being affable and well-liked, and capable 85 percent of the time, lately has affected team productivity in a negative way.

The Wrong Move. Make accusatory or "you" statements.
The Consequence. The employee will clam up, putting the responsibility on you to take the next step.
The Right Move. Ask a series of questions and listen carefully: you'll find out whether the problem is with the affable but struggling employee, or whether your judgment is completely off base. It's possible, for example, that external obstacles are to blame.

SUMMING UP

As much as possible, your operating structure should give people a sense of control. People want control over their environment and how they do their work certainly, but they also need to know that to some extent they can control or at least influence the bigger picture. A good approach to decision making is essential to your goal of sharing responsibility and control.

In guiding your team to making smart individual decisions, consider whether they are using the right structure and processes. If you feel they are not, address this, and help them find better ways of appropriate decision making. It's important that you help the individuals on the team understand that you are not at work to be in a parent–child relationship.

Your expectations about responsible behavior must be clear, and this should lead in a straight line to their personal on-the-job decisions and their participation in the group's direction.

Chapter 8

MANAGING ON A HOPE
AND A PRAYER

Real Life

Fortune (June 21, 1999) in its article "Why CEOs Fail," estimated that 70 percent of the time the real problem behind leadership failure is not the high-level concepts and strategies the team rallies behind, but rather the result of *bad execution*: not getting things done, indecisiveness, and failure to deliver on commitments. Leaders also fail when they don't put the right people in the right jobs, and then they make it all worse by failing to fix people problems in time.

But most importantly, leaders fail because they lack the emotional strength to listen to their "inner voice" and recognize a problem of sustained poor performance. As the leader, you need to monitor your team's performance and the results, and you need to make any required changes to the process or the people. Failing to get this part of your job right puts the whole organization and all its stakeholders at risk.

AN ACCOUNTABLE PROCESS LEADS TO CONSISTENT TOP PERFORMANCE

Structurally speaking, preventing poor performance, and unintended results, requires that you effectively set and manage expectations of the team and its individual members. That requires thoughtful planning of an accountable process with a consistent, well-articulated structure, a method of measurement and an ongoing comparison of actual results to the Plan; in short, achievement of goals.

Some Personal Insights: Spelling Bees and Gold Stars

There are many who would argue that competition among team members or individuals on the team—particularly in a work environment—is bad. We don't want the bright lights to overshadow the others, is the general reasoning. We would rather celebrate the consistently average. While there is no doubt that coming up to the norm is a challenge for some and a great accomplishment, the most energizing exercise for the majority is an environment with an edge.

Think back for a moment to the spelling bees of old, those who came in second often strove to come in first the next time. With one little gold star after another, consistent excellence became tangible, and important. Kids learned to study with purpose and to enjoy the recognition and the rewards.

Performance markers work, even for adults. They spur people on to stretch and reach for the top.

In the workplace today, we find that when we set goals for achievement and chart them, we not only get the results but quite often surpass them. Your expectations for the team and its members will generally require two types of markers.

- Assessment of the activities and results directly related to the bottom line
- Assessment of behavior and attitudes as they relate to the mission and values of the team

The first criteria is largely definable and measurable, and the latter is more subjective. Both are necessary to get the results you want and need.

When you set achievement goals you facilitate a direct path to an important by-product: personal satisfaction and happiness.

Tools such as job descriptions, performance plans linked with ongoing discussions, project plans, team-based annual plans, one-on-one meetings, meeting agendas, and follow-up sessions, can all be used to assist in clearly articulating and tracking your expectations of the team and its members.

WRITTEN JOB DESCRIPTIONS AND PERFORMANCE PLANS

In theory, writing down what a new employee is supposed to do in his role (a job description), and what he is expected to achieve in the coming year (a performance plan), sounds like an excellent idea. In practice, these tools often contain flowery and vague language (likely a cut-and-paste job from another document) and do not nail down exactly what is expected of the individual. For fear of missing some small element of the overall responsibility, these tools sometimes become verbose documents typically filed away and not to be consulted again until the end of the year.

In reality, what are the *results* you want and need from the planning process for each team member? This is your most important question before you begin to work with an employee for whom you have the responsibility of assessment. What does he or she really need to accomplish? What type of "teammanship" is expected of the role?

TEAM-BASED ROLE DESCRIPTIONS

The problem can be resolved if you are willing to set aside previous job descriptions and performance plans, take a blank sheet of paper and provide a role description. Write down exactly:

- What the person needs to do (essential functions and activities)
- What the outcomes need to be (accountable functions and results)
- Who will be interacting with this person (team members and supervisors)

Better still, ask the employee to do this with you once you have communicated the results you need to achieve. If you have recruited well, this person likely brings with him or her strengths and aptitudes based on past experience that can result in new and positive changes for the team. *Discuss the potential contribution of fresh ideas with new team members and implement them into the role.*

In writing new role descriptions and in particular in clearly describing the key accountabilities, avoid the use of corporate jargon and ask yourself, *what really needs to be done for this person to be successful?* There are likely a couple of items that are particularly important, and these essential responsibilities must be crystal clear in the document and to the individual.

Resisting the temptation to recycle previous job descriptions and performance plans requires more time and effort in the short term, but it will help you down the road if there is a gap between the expectations and the actual outcome. This is particularly important in changing environments, and in team-based projects, which depend upon a "blurred line" approach to getting things done. That is, in order for the team to make a decision about who does what and when, a simple focus on a team member's primary—rather than exact—role provides a clear, direct line to successful results.

Here is an example:

At today's opportunity weekly team meeting, Sally in sales reported that a client contacted the company to request a volume discount for a product over a limited period, and the client asked whether we would be interested in producing a hard-copy insert detailing the offer and providing a purchase application form for insertion in their next newsletter at the end of the month. The team agreed this was a great opportunity.

Collaboration on role assignment: After a project planning process is completed, the team members together agree on who will do what, determining that Sally in sales should own the project and take responsibility for preparing the detailed project plan and seeing it through. Tom in the art department would draft up a version of our current promotional package and customize it to meet the client's specifications. Jon in compliance would review hard and soft copy for accuracy as well as privacy and legal requirements. Marcia in administration would prepare the budget and purchase orders for postage, stationery, electronic file distribution, and printing. Debbie in shipping would be notified of the delivery date so that she could prepare the mailing.

Knowing the primary role descriptions and accountabilities of each person on the team makes it easy for the right individuals to assign themselves to the appropriate aspects of the project and create implementation plans that make sense and will be achieved.

Rote scanning through detailed lists to find out whether an activity was on the job description for a particular person is not productive. In our experience, rote job descriptions no longer work, especially if you expect your employees to embrace a new approach to meaningful work:

- A participative management role
- An opportunity to develop leadership skills
- A chance to engage their "whole brain" toward creative solutions
- The use of their unique skill sets and experience

Setting up a team to operate in this fashion means that the company benefits from every employee's intelligence, ideas, and creativity for the advancement of corporate goals. Most importantly, each individual has the opportunity to do meaningful work.

PROJECT PLANS AND PERIODIC REPORTING

Formal reporting processes and forms are required to clarify performance expectations for your team, and these are an important tool to keep your weekly team meetings focused as well. Weekly reporting by each team member should entail the following:

- What were your performance goals this week?
- Were they achieved? Explain why or why not.
- What was the key messaging from the marketplace or constituency we serve?
- Were there any obstacles?
- What are next week's goals?

Examples of Information to Be Gathered and Reported

Sales
- Inquiries this year and last year (+ or −)
- Percent turned to sales this year and last year (+ or −)
- Total revenue earned this year and last year
- Cost per inquiry
- Cost per sales
- Plan to budget results

Marketing
- Projects completed last week
- New projects for this week
- Cost of new promotional activity
- Plan to budget results

Quality
- Client issues this week compared to same time last year
- Key problems and successes with product use

- Solutions required
- Plan to budget results

Product Development
- Client issues solved last week compared to issues this week
- New product enhancement proposals
- Proposed new intellectual properties
- Plan to budget results

Depending on the nature of your team's responsibilities, reporting documents may set out the overall team goals (such as sales and revenue) versus results. Or the information may be a project plan spreadsheet itemizing the specific projects that require completion, with individual responsibilities and deadlines assigned in the document, again by team agreement. As well as providing clarity to everyone, they bring purpose to the meeting and allow team members to solve problems, forming the basis for fruitful strategic thinking and planning at every regular weekly meeting. These reports develop the habit of discussing results, ensuring accountability as team characteristic. Good, bad, or indifferent, reviewing individual accomplishments will become a regular event, resulting in greater engagement and responsiveness and an opportunity for everyone to have an impact on the business and its stakeholders.

There is also plenty of opportunity for team coaching—not just by the leader, but by all team members. *People start working at their full potential and are more apt to deliver on their commitments when they understand the importance of their work to everyone else on the team.*

The outdated alternative to a systematic reporting process, of course, is to review results only when the team, or some member of the team, is underperforming; however, if your goal is to *minimize* the times you need to "tell it like it is," and keep fires off your desk, it is far better to put a process in place that prevents underperforming from occurring.

There is still a place for periodic or annual performance reviews and planning retreats. However, here too you may wish to make that process more collaborative and engage your team in planning for results in the future or in analyzing new directions. This will help your team understand your obligations and responsibilities better and the importance of their performance as it relates to your team's ability to succeed.

DAILY REINFORCING CHATS

Even more important and relevant than periodic performance reviews is the guidance you can provide through daily reinforcing chats that keep your team on track. In defining how you interact with individual members of your team, consider the following:

- How do I encourage an environment which provides people with the freedom to make a choice about their personal time and health, while meeting expectations at work?
- How can I help people put work into perspective with their stage of life?
- If leaders are made, not born, how can I use the opportunity of individual meetings to help people further develop their leadership careers?

MEETING MINUTES: TEAM AND ONE ON ONE

A trap for leaders is a failure to follow up, yet consistent follow-up can quickly become the expected norm, to the great advantage of Plan delivery. Meeting minutes are important, and team members should rotate responsibility for writing and distributing them. Make it clear that this record of what was agreed to does not need to be fency.

After individual meetings, a quick e-mail from you can summarize your understanding of what was discussed and agreed upon as well as provide definite dates for tasks to be done or results achieved. When this is done regularly and immediately following a meeting, there is an additional benefit for you: it sends the message that this is simply how you work as a leader and is not a reflection of a lack of trust.

When you follow up only when there is a problem or on an irregular basis, any one-on-one communication from you will signal disapproval or crisis management.

MEANINGFUL REWARDS

It often seems that there is little time for celebration when expectations are met, given restraints of time and money. Yet when the individuals on a team do come together as one united front, achieving their goals, the most effective reward structures provide both the team and the individual with recognition and either financial or nonfinancial benefits. Rewards can be centered around:

- Success in execution of the Plan
- Success in innovation and collaboration
- Success in adapting to change
- Dedication to customer responsiveness
- Leadership in living a balanced lifestyle

Note that we refer to "financial or nonfinancial benefits." To some people, money is the preferred benefit at all times, but to others, no reward is as great as the luxury of time. New rewards that may motivate people include time, educational opportunities, or health and well-being programs. It is important for leaders today to think beyond the traditional reward and recognition structures if the intention is to maximize their motivational impact.

SUMMING UP

While managers and workplaces in general today may *appear* to be much more tolerant and understanding, the bottom line must still be achieved. It is up to the leader to find the tools and processes that will make this happen, as well as the rewards and recognition that will further motivate the team to succeed.

Chapter 9

THEY'LL DO WHAT YOU DO, NOT WHAT YOU SAY

Real Life

Writing a mission statement together, having a daylong meeting away from the office, or even going on a retreat are all pointless if the leader does not, through daily words *and* actions, make it clear what really matters. In other words, the right structure and processes will only work with regular and consistent reinforcing communications and follow-up from the leader. Whether the team operates in a bank or a kiosk, before any type of process can be put in place, the leader's job is to convey what really matters.

What matters? Consider these "clues":

- The executive offices of some financial services companies have monitors in prominent places tracking minute-by-minute earnings.
- Professionals track billable time in six-minute intervals.
- Retail franchises typically have software enabling the CFO or even CEO in the head office to check the daily (or more frequent) sales in each store.

> • In the most successful coffee kiosks, you will see a person, clearly the owner, at the cash register, greeting customers, watching the cream and sugar booths for cleanliness, scrambling to fix the order of the customer who got a latte instead of the cappuccino she ordered.
>
> What matters...is whatever is going to drive the bottom line and the referral of the next new customer to your business.

The old saying, "Do as I say, not as I do," immediately comes to mind. Even though it is vitally important to be explicit and clear when stating expectations, a leader's actions are equally, if not more, important. While a well-worded role description is useful to a new employee and a written performance plan at the outset of every year is also a good idea, these explicit statements (often reading like statements praising motherhood and apple pie) are outweighed in importance by the day-in, day-out demonstrations by leaders of their expectations.

INFLUENCING BEHAVIOR

We assume that sales clerks who say neither "please" nor "thank you" to paying customers have at some point been advised, verbally or in writing, that customer service is important. But they have not likely had repeated exposure to their leader or manager serving customers in a friendly, respectful manner. It is the *leader* whose personal attitudes and behavior primarily shape the team's attitudes and behavior. A team observes whether or not a leader does what he says, and says what he does, and for good or bad, a team will usually follow suit. The more senior the leader's position, the greater the need for him or her to get it right in terms of impressions; the corporate grapevine quickly conveys stories of what the top boss says, does, and thinks.

An example of this is sometimes seen when annual employee attitude surveys result in the start of new initiatives to address problems. If a "lack of communication" is raised, a leader may throw his weight behind lunch-and-learn sessions, employee break-fasts, or newsletters, all designed to enhance the communication in the company. Although these may be worthwhile ideas, when the leader or senior management team are absent from these gath-erings after the kickoff session, or the newsletter becomes one more thing for the administrative assistant to produce, the processes put in place, while ostensibly useful, soon lose their vitality.

There is no easy answer to this. It would be naïve to suggest that the VP of marketing should attend the lunch-and-learn session if the ad agency just called to announce that the multimillion-dollar campaign launched that day is fatally flawed. Every leader's job is demanding and it is important to focus on what really needs to be done. We simply note that if a leader's actions, over time, con-sistently contradict his or her words, there will eventually be no process left. Even where the leader demonstrates full commitment to any particular team process, if most people on the team view it a waste of time, the interest and participation of the team will slip away. To avoid this, in implementing a process, ask yourself:

- How does the process link to the strategic initiative? Any pro-cess you create should assist in executing tactical goals linked to specific results.
- Have I included the team in deciding on this process?
- Have I included people outside the team who may be inter-ested in, or affected by, the process?
- Why do we need the process? Do I believe in the value of the process or am I implementing it because I am being told to do so or because "it seems like" a good idea? If so, is there another way to structure the mandated process that I would find more useful? If so, do it.
- Who should be involved? Would implementation of the process be a job-enriching activity for a member of the team, or is there a way in which implementation could be shared among the team?
- Does the process provide the results I need? Does it allow us to focus on what is important?

UNCONSCIOUS INFLUENCE

The leader's influence is keenly felt in how she manages herself within the team's structure. For example, let's say that the team has decided to run its weekly update meetings on a tight schedule with each person presenting last week's sales and the coming week's prospects and activities. However, in the meetings the leader often interrupts, raising points that are on her own mind and taking the meeting off its planned track. While seeming innocent—after all, she is the boss and what is on her mind is clearly important—this behavior can have detrimental consequences:

1. **Process is undermined.** The agreed-on process is undermined, as is the team's belief that their input into process-related decisions is valued.
2. **Participation will wane.** Participation in the meeting is likely reduced, particularly from those team members who by role or by seniority may feel that their contributions cannot possibly be at the same level as the boss's agenda items.
3. **New leadership opportunities are lost.** The opportunity to grant team members informal or transitory leadership is lost or minimized, because of the leader's implicit emphasis on her leadership position.
4. **Rules of respectful behavior are compromised.** The opportunity to show respect to those in attendance who have more junior roles, or roles whose contribution may not be regularly feted in the company, is lost, as the leader chooses to use the meeting primarily for her agenda.

When these types of "interferences" are made by the leader, the impact is typically inconsequential on senior people around the table and highly important to those with less power. Senior team members with their own power and position will be mildly irritated and go back to their offices muttering about the boss always taking over the sales meeting. If generally speaking, the boss is a good leader, her inclination to ignore team processes will not be a big deal. This is likely why some meetings at very senior levels can be raucous affairs, completely off the agenda at times, and yet still effective: all participants are confident and articulate and have no problem getting their message across, even if they are not the most senior person at the table.

On the other hand, in the more usual case, a team includes a variety of roles and several levels of seniority and perceived importance. It is essential to use such team meetings as opportunities to give aspiring leaders a voice and to show respect to those team members in roles occasionally referred to as "support" or "administrative," which are typically perceived as less glamorous than positions in sales or managing client relationships. Not undermining the process is a critical factor in encouraging a team to question what is going on, to take risks, and ultimately to create an opportunity conducive to developing new leaders.

With ambitious team members who see themselves progressing rapidly, it may be challenging for a leader to satisfy their needs through actual promotions in a time frame that matches their expectations. Armed with one or more degrees and a lot of confidence, they see themselves in the CEO position some day... soon. Therefore, it is essential that a team process be built (*and followed*) to place these individuals into leadership roles, defined as providing opportunities to speak up, be listened to, and feel like an equal at the table. No matter how confident he or she may be, however, that willingness to participate may be eroded if suddenly the leader is, well, acting like the leader all the time.

Similar but different, are the essential team members who provide administrative or technical support to the team and who may be, in some cases, a little shy or quiet. Being *told* that a meeting is their opportunity to speak up and participate fully will usually mean absolutely nothing once the process is hijacked by the boss or, frankly, by any more senior team member. Here, what is lost is the chance to make the supportive team members really feel like a part of the team, contributors. Without that feeling, speeches about being off the sales plan, or "under plan" will mean nothing to them, and they will not seek to find solutions or assist the team in getting back on track, even though there are very likely many ways in which they could do just that. Why? Because the day-to-day processes, such as participative team meetings, *as interpreted by senior management*, do not indicate that these team members really matter. The result? The fires keep popping up on *your* desk, causing stress, waste, and mismanagement of resources.

SUMMING UP

There is no single perfect structure or process to ensure your team's success, but in our experience, a team is most likely to achieve its Plan if its structure provides:

1. A high degree of communication among all stakeholders to the team's results.
2. Formal, accountable reporting processes.
3. The dissemination and discussion of important strategic initiatives.
4. Ongoing (daily) individual and team coaching.
5. Traditional and nontraditional recognition and rewards for both the team and its members.

Never underestimate your impact as leader to get the best out of people. Show the way, by presenting opportunities for each individual to leave their comfort zone and participate in leadership.

Do It Yourself

Responsibility 2: The Team Structure

- **Lead with a big-picture perspective.** Understand who is affected by and interested in your team's results and activities, and be sure that you and the team keep the "team-around-the-team" in mind when planning your strategies.
- **Don't permit an Us versus Them attitude in your team.** Everyone on the team has an important role to play or

they shouldn't be there. Find ways to involve, include, and consult with every team member.

- **Share information freely.** What's the big secret? The more information you share with your team, the more they will feel part of the team's purpose.
- **Encourage your team to welcome communications and information.** Get everyone involved in harnessing these sources and maximizing your internal processes so they don't become overwhelming.
- **Consider the factors in decision making before making them all yourself.** People will support decisions that they have had a say in making far more than those in which they were not consulted.
- **Be relentless in following up.** Failure in leadership most often results from just not carrying through on achievable tasks. You only become a micromanager if you follow up after a team member has demonstrated consistent ability to get things done.
- **Convey every day what really matters.** Where you focus your time and energy, and how you govern your words and actions, will largely determine the actions and attitudes of your team.

RESPONSIBILITY 3

THE PLAN

*"The ending is everything. Plan all the way to it,
taking into account all the possible consequences,
obstacles and twists of fortune that might reverse
your hard work... By planning to the end you will
not be overwhelmed by circumstances and you will know
when to stop. Gently guide fortune and help determine
the future by thinking far ahead."*

Robert Greene,
The 48 Laws of Power

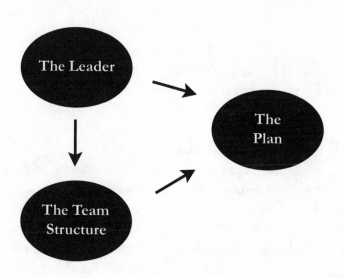

Real Life

One of the biggest challenges of leadership is being able at all times to articulate with clarity the team's direction and also the specific expectations for it, its Plan.

The effective leader will never accept ambiguous goals such as: *Your team needs to do more with less this year.* How much more with how much less? If no one can answer that question, the team can never be successful; *those sought-after productivity goals will not happen.* Never hide behind generalities. Insist on clarity: we need to have 300 stores earning $xxx in sales by August of xxxx. How will we get there? People can break down and deal with clear expectations.

Meeting your Plan is about consistently living up to expectations. This requires clarity and precision around desired outcomes. The strong leader never responds, "Yes, boss," to a request to "do better." You'll find your team heading directly down the wrong path to everyone's unpleasant surprise.

Responsibility 3, The Plan, discusses how to correctly ascertain your team's objectives, and then proceed to use your Plan as the anchor for your team's work.

THE NONNEGOTIABLES

A successful leader recognizes that achieving certain specific results is simply nonnegotiable. However, what sounds simple is not easy and is usually the main reason why a leader fails: he or she was unable to lead the team to achieve its primary objectives, a scorecard of must-haves that we will refer to simply as *the Plan*. The irony is that often an unsuccessful leader has the *ability* to lead the team to achieve its Plan, but cannot recognize the essential tasks in the Plan, or having understood the Plan initially, does not keep focused on its attainment. *If the leader is not focused on the right goals, there is little or no chance of success, regardless of team effort.*

One reason for this type of failure in leadership is the sheer volume of communication that hits leaders in any type of organization every day. On top of just being plain distracting, the "noise" created by this onslaught often makes noncore tasks appear more important than they really are. Coupled with the numerous demands on the leader's time to be involved in an unlimited number of "good things," it is easy to be unwittingly knocked off track. Usually there are fewer than six of these nonnegotiable objectives for a team to achieve. There may also be reams of other negotiable goals, but typically there are not a lot of absolutely essential ones. Having a plan and a process for sticking to it helps sort the nonnegotiables from the negotiables.

Stephen Covey's book, *First Things First Every Day*, uses an analogy involving a jar which needs to contain as much rocks, gravel, sand, and water as possible. If the rocks represent the really essential tasks or goals for each individual, Covey points out that the only way to be sure to achieve them is to place them in the jar before the other elements are added: trying to push rocks into a jar already filled with gravel and sand is a far more difficult exercise than putting the large stones in first. This is good advice for every individual challenged with time management.

For team leaders, however, the importance of ascertaining and pursuing the right key objectives is multiplied by the number of people on the team. If the leader is off-focus, chances are that his or her team will be too. The team then quickly loses ground in a competitive environment.

SUMMING UP

As a leader, you need to have your eye on achieving the Plan—putting the big rocks in the jar first. You must also know how to lead the team through the inevitable changes that will arise during execution, when the jar proves to be too small to maximize the opportunities in the marketplace.

Chapter 10

I'M NOT SURE WHAT I'M DOING, BUT I'M DOING IT WELL

Real Life

The manager requires a focus on the big picture (the future), as well as a clear understanding of the goals and actionable objectives that will bring it all together (the present). In fact, one could argue that middle managers are the most important component of corporate success because they are the ones that make it all come together. Positioned between the executives of the organization who provide strategic direction and the people who serve both the internal and external world, middle managers are the ones who drive performance of the company as a whole, and manage the available resources. Having the right corporate strategies is important, but the key to the organization's success is your stewardship around the resourceful and timely execution of the Plan.

MAKE IT YOUR PLAN

For middle managers who are handed a Plan by the next management level up in the organization, the essential task (and this is where you have control and influence) is devising a viable strategy to achieve the Plan. Although the Plan itself is nonnegotiable—it must be delivered—you will likely be given quite a bit of latitude in deciding how to achieve it. To develop a successful strategy, you must be able to:

1. **Guard resources.** As a steward of your company's financial and human resources you must be able to budget, cut costs if required, and recruit and retain great people.
2. **Execute with purpose.** You must continuously clarify the team's purpose and ensure that the team members are equipped to achieve it.
3. **Communicate extremely well.** You must be able to effectively disseminate information about the Plan to the team, consistently come back to it, and provoke strategic thinking within your team on how to achieve the results you want.
4. **Manage internal and external relationships.** You must keep your eye on the many relationships which are important to your team, recognizing new opportunities through communication with clients and other parties who are influential to your team's success.
5. **Become an agent of change.** You must be able to reallocate resources on the fly to take advantage of opportunities as they arrive, assessing your team's skills, teaching new skills, and acquiring new talent with strong skills and fresh perspectives.
6. **Establish a culture of innovative thinking.** You must inspire creativity and confidence in your team by always encouraging new ideas and processes.

Keeping the team focused on achieving its Plan, those defined objectives required for your team to succeed, is arguably the most important aspect of leadership. Success against the Plan plays a significant role in both the viability of the team and the satisfaction of its members. It is your responsibility to know the Plan cold, both from a financial and human resource point of view, enabling you to:

- **Create a culture conducive to individual and team decision making.** When the team understands the Plan and appreciates its importance, you improve the ability for your team to make decisions about current issues on the fly. They are then able to better control their workloads by taking a direct approach to problem solving. Always ask your team to consider: "What results do we want?" or "Will this help me get the results I want?" If they are unclear about what results they want or need, you must assist them by revisiting the Plan and their individual role in its achievement.

- **Set up a structure and process for communicating results.** Accountability—through formal weekly reporting to the team, for example—provides purpose and control. Each person learns to measure him or herself against the Plan and is motivated to meet the deadline set by the team.

- **Get connected with the team members regularly.** The Plan is the driver of these communications: talk about common goals and achievements, celebrate when things happen on Plan, and regroup when they don't. The best leaders are not afraid to roll up their sleeves in good or bad times—something that earns them lasting respect from everyone.

- **Follow up on every commitment your direct reports make to you.** Your job is not to do their jobs . . . your job is to guide them to achieving the right results. This means you have to know what their role is on the team and as an individual and help them when lines are blurred and performance objectives are hazy. Don't miss any follow-up opportunities: if you tell a team member that his or her weekly update with you is every Monday morning at 9:30, nothing is more important. Should you have to miss this meeting, it is critical that you apologize and reschedule. Sticking to scheduled meetings with agendas always tying back to the Plan develops a culture of participative management.

- **Be very wary when everything is rosy.** The best companies face bad news every day. If you aren't hearing anything that disturbs you, chances are you have a communication breakdown, beginning with you. Be proactive and find out what's brewing, and ask yourself why you are not hearing both good and bad news. Are people intimidated by you? Do they not trust you to keep your cool? Will you point fingers in a crisis rather than help sort matters out? Find out the problem and correct it.

Some Personal Insights on Personal Contact and Clarity

Technology is great, but nothing beats personal contact. When two e-mails don't get the job done, pick up the phone, or meet in person, and find out why. There is no better and more valuable opportunity than to be able to have a clear meeting of the minds over an issue that requires deeper thought. Never rely on e-mail to do that for you. You'll miss the warm feeling of serving your client/employee/associate/boss in the most effective way of all—with your personal attention.

USE YOUR BETTER JUDGMENT AND SET QUANTIFIABLE TARGETS

Achieving the objectives and staying focused are things that may seem obvious and even trite; yet pitfalls are common. The first challenge is to have a firm understanding of what items are on the Plan and what items are not. You may be thinking, how can a leader possibly *mis*understand what his or her assigned Plan really is?

The challenge comes from the *quantity* of expectations that are now placed on a leader, at every level of an organization. The leader who assesses every one of these expectations as bearing equal weight will burn out the team. However, the decision to give the wrong objectives too much weight will almost surely result in failure.

The following is an example: Throughout Gillian's recruitment to a managerial position, the hiring executives frequently referred to the team's low morale and the need for the new manager to turn that around. Upon starting, Gillian focused with laserlike intensity on addressing employee concerns and making everyone feel better. But at the end of the first fiscal year, the team had failed to achieve its sales targets, and Gillian found that the newly implemented employee initiatives did not garner the accolades (or the bonus) that she had expected.

Although Gillian did exactly what she was asked to do she had overlooked that the fundamental task of the team—the Plan—was to achieve a certain level of sales. The hiring managers had assumed that as a "given" and had mentioned the team morale as a side item that they had assumed would improve as the team became more successful.

WHAT TO DO TO START AND STAY ON PLAN

In the face of so many expectations on you and your team, some suggestions for figuring out what is really important (and therefore comprises your Plan) are (1) ask, (2) verify, (3) assess, and (4) consult.

Ask

This may seem obvious but it is often overlooked, at least as a direct question. Asking the boss (which may mean a senior executive in a corporate setting and a bank or investors in a small business) can be very insightful into what really matters most.

Remember, it's your job to achieve the Plan, so you had better be sure you have it right. Your boss is going to expect the following from you:

- **A full understanding** of the business and your role in the stewardship of its resources
- **An ability to lead and develop your team** in the context of the Plan, measure their performance, and retain top talent
- **Sharing of information,** when appropriate and expected, both up and down the ranks, and the ability to listen carefully for feedback from above and below
- **A process for monitoring activity and diagnosing problems** relating to internal and external stakeholders as well as the ability to define whether team members are working at their maximum potential for Plan achievement

Verify: Is Your Boss Sure?

It is also important that the length of the laundry list you are assigned is discussed openly. Numerous requests to achieve different targets (sales, compliance matter, hiring, etc.) are made at different times, from different stakeholders, with the result that even senior management sometimes does not fully grasp the splintered efforts that may result. Since every requirement on a lengthy list can simply not be met, you need to ascertain: *What matters most?* Sometimes the clearest way to express what you are asking is: "What will affect my performance rating and bonus?" Factors affecting your personal compensation clearly reflect what your team must achieve.

Assess the Environment

Particularly in an entrepreneurial situation, formulating and delivering the right Plan requires an accurate understanding of the competitive landscape. One approach is to follow a series of defined steps to achieving the Plan and managing your risk:

1. Draw a straight line to the results you need to get to be successful (as defined by your desired income or requirements of lenders and investors).
2. Gather historical facts about previous similar undertakings and businesses in the field.
3. Research the competitive landscape.
4. Understand the knowledge gaps you may have.
5. Float some trial balloons with mentors or investors on your board.
6. Prepare an analysis that identifies and quantifies risk to the following resources:
   - Available human capital: Do you have enough people with the right skill-sets?
   - Your supply chain: Will your suppliers be able to meet your demands and on time?
   - Financial resources: Will financing or other costs rise in the near future, affecting profitability?
   - Changes in regulatory, political, or other external environments: How will these changes affect your Plan?

Consult a Peer or Mentor

People who are successful in a similar job can be invaluable in helping you sort the wheat from the chaff. Although still only one opinion, high achievers are often self-confident people who are more than happy to describe at length what they see as their most important objectives. Consider these discussion points:

- **What is rewarded.** Occasionally the message given to external parties about what a team does is different from what is actually expected. For example, a travel company can have as its hallmark (both internally and externally) the delivery of an integrated offering to clients—an all-encompassing business and personal travel service—but if the rules to win are designed to favor those who sell business travel, then that is a clear signal as to what really matters.

- **Negative outcomes.** Thinking ahead to possible consequences of not delivering on an expectation can sometimes move it onto the critical list. A good example of this are the expectations about compliance and risk management. At times these areas seem dull, boring, and not central to the team's success in the same way as the sales targets. But what are the ramifications of a shoddy audit by the external regulators or a major fraud being perpetrated in your department? The point is that some expectations need to be looked at in terms of not delivering them: What would happen then? The answer may compel you to pay more attention.

- **Really know the numbers.** It is one thing to say that the sales and revenue targets are essential and another matter to immerse yourself in the details and understand key items, such as how different types of sales translate into revenue (is revenue affected by interest rates or foreign exchange?) and the costs associated with some sales over others, due to varying levels of travel expenses and commission structures. Could you explain to a person on the street, uninformed on your business, the underlying components of the Plan, the Plan itself, and the key drivers (activities) that will be required to achieve it? If not, perhaps some further analysis and number-crunching is required.

Your peer or mentor may have personal experiences to add in helping you focus on these three critical points.

SUMMING UP

In most businesses, the common feature in the Plan is the net income statement for the year ahead, but if your team is in operations and compliance, for example, its Plan may instead be composed of different quantitative benchmarks against which its performance is measured, such as field audit outcomes, client satisfaction surveys, and cost control. Even if your Plan is primarily focused on some key sales, productivity, and profitability targets, it may also include some very important secondary items, such as referrals to other areas of the company (in a multiple-channel sales operation, for example) and successful audits by both internal and external auditors, the latter example being increasingly part of a leader's Plan in the wake of large corporate frauds.

Whatever makes up your Plan, whatever truly matters to the organization and your boss, you need to know it cold and be adept at explaining it perfectly anytime, anywhere.

Chapter 11

EVERY BEACH HAS A LINE IN THE SAND

Real Life

Three things are key: the fact that you have impact with your team, that you plan well, and that you anticipate what is to come. Your boss expects you to understand what it is you and your team must do, how to produce results, and how to implement a methodical yet flexible process in anticipation of changes or barriers. You must move the work forward from conception to completion on an ongoing basis. You are the link between corporate direction and employee execution and your job is to plan to make things happen, on time.

Once you are crystal clear on what the team needs to do to succeed, you begin the communication process. The team needs to hear from you what the nonnegotiable requirements are—exactly what must be achieved and the benchmarks you will be using to measure performance.

To work in tandem toward the same result, you and your team must be on the same page. It helps if everyone knows the Plan, and that's your job. To instill an understanding in the team of the essential elements of the Plan, consider the following steps to successful communication and implementation:

- **Preview the Plan.** An up front review of the materials you have been given, including more information than you strictly need to share, demonstrates your trust in the team. Be transparent and share the information and background details that you receive as the leader. There is little to be gained by keeping people in the dark.
- **Determine reporting requirements.** Development of specific reports that will sift through all the available data and clearly set out the most important information.
- **Present Plan markers.** Communication of a scorecard that contains the key elements of the Plan that is produced and circulated weekly or monthly to everyone on the team.
- **Create a buzz around results.** Creation of a focal point for recording success against the Plan, for example, a prominently displayed graph of the team's key results to build momentum.
- **Design rewards and recognition programs.** Choose the right variables so that there is no confusion as to what counts and is measured.

BALANCING THE PLAN AS A TEAM

It is outdated thinking to assume that delivery of the Plan must be accomplished in a certain way. Extending your team members some autonomy in determining this for themselves will almost certainly pay off in gains in your team's commitment. The only requirements for making this work are to:

- **Ensure that you are confident** with what the Plan is, for example, how much leeway do you have in extending to individuals the ability to design their work time and workplace?
- **Monitor the results** of these arrangements against achievement of the Plan. Ideally if you have successfully communicated

the Plan and its importance to the team, when the results against Plan are not there, team members will recognize that changes need to be made, perhaps including changes to the flexibility they have enjoyed to date. However, even if individuals do not assess the situation correctly, it is up to you to once again refer to the Plan as the reason for a change.

- **Manage personal choices and priorities**. When everyone on the team knows what is negotiable and what is not, *and why*, the response to special requests arising daily—for example, to leave early each day to accommodate the daycare—is a simple question: What impact does this request (or behavior) have on the Plan? If the request cannot be met without negatively affecting the team's necessary output, then the answer is obvious, not because you are a mean boss but simply because the team's primary responsibility is to deliver the Plan.

  Make it clear that you are *paying for results*, not time on the job. If it is possible to combine an individual's preferences about where, how, and when they work, then those desires should be carefully considered. No one wants the team to burn out or good people to leave. Often the best way to encourage your team toward a well-balanced life, while working with a focus on results, is simply to demonstrate these attributes in your own life.

Your specific focus on a team member's personal life is required whenever you sense the existence of an addiction or an otherwise unmanageable personal or family life, or begin to observe chronic absenteeism or unethical behavior. To the extent that your corporate infrastructure offers resources to help the individual get back on track, it is important to assist him or her in accessing this help. These challenges cannot threaten the team and its overall attainment of the Plan. It is neither fair to the rest of the team nor the reality of corporate life to permit one individual to derail the team. Your job is to neutralize the effects on the team, sooner rather than later.

SUMMING UP

Sometimes business objectives and plans can be complicated and lengthy, involving many different factors that will affect the ease or difficulty of achievement. Regardless of your Plan's complexity, we can't emphasize enough how important it is for team members to fully appreciate what the nonnegotiable items are when it comes to their combined and individual performance and results. The team will focus where you focus, and that focus cannot be a mystery.

Chapter 12

A SALARY FOR YOUR THOUGHTS

Real Life

Your individual team members will *not* have a sense of true ownership of their Plan unless they are granted an opportunity to participate in figuring out the strategy to achieve it. We often hear about the importance of positive feedback, and as we ourselves suggest throughout the book, providing recognition for accomplishments is an essential part of a leader's job. But think of those times when *you* felt most appreciated, trusted, and valued; likely these occasions included times when you were asked to provide your ideas and advice. Often, asking others for their thoughts is the best feedback of all: you value what they have to say. For your team's greatest success, find ways to extend opportunities for involvement and input to the people on your team.

Whether you are a business owner or a leader in a public company, you have the opportunity to take the Plan to your team for their involvement. Work with the team to devise a strategic vision for the Plan's implementation and execution and in so doing remind each individual of the belief you have in the value of their contributions.

Part of the process of asking people to participate is to share your own knowledge and experience. There is no point keeping it to yourself. As a leader, make it easy for your team members to discuss ideas and don't be afraid to share what you know and think with them. The most successful teams are Plan-based but operate as ongoing open forums for new ideas, new processes, and new ways to achieve the Plan.

A PLAN FOR ENGAGEMENT

If you have ever wondered why people are willing to work long hours for terrible pay in building a start-up company, reflect on this: the freedom to excel, the ability to control when and how things are done, and the opportunity for personal significance are often more important to top performers than a corner office and a six-figure salary. How can you help your team become top performers? The answer can be summed up in one word: *Engagement.*

In order to engage your whole team's full commitment to the Plan, you need a strategy that has been designed by everyone on the team. Since each team's strategy will be unique, there is not one single way to develop it; however, points to keep in mind include:

- **Start early.** The most successful leaders and their teams are working on their strategy several months before the end of the current year. In other words, waiting for the boss (head office, the bank, investors) to tell you exactly what needs to be accomplished in the year ahead is too late. You should be able to estimate the key expectations which will be set for the team based on prior years' plans and extrapolate into the future to enable the team to begin its planning process well ahead of the pack.
- **Encourage participation.** Devising the action plan to achieve expectations ("Plan A") requires that everyone is

involved in the process. If your team members also lead people, find ways in which the wider team can be included in the process. If a person is on the team, then by definition that person has a role to play in the team's success or failure, so his or her views should be obtained and considered.

- **Identify barriers to success.** The old fashioned SWOT analysis is worth doing every time the team develops its plans: Strengths, Weaknesses, Opportunities, and Threats. Insist on looking underneath the rocks and encourage the team to imagine the worst. Then devise a contingency plan ("Plan B"). Most importantly, make it clear that you are not a leader who only needs or wants to hear the sugar-coated versions.

- **Don't leap to the first options or solutions.** Have an open mind. As an experienced leader, you may be particularly inclined to form a strategy in your mind as you were initially reviewing and confirming the Plan. Try to avoid prematurely closing discussions; you will risk losing excellent ideas.

- **Address accountabilities and timelines.** People need as much clarity as possible, and the planning meetings are the first opportunity to begin assigning the what, when, and who of the Plan execution. Subsequent one-on-one meetings will be the primary opportunity to agree on and convey individual objectives, but it is never too early to begin clarifying expectations and defining individual role requirements as a team.

- **Plan to succeed.** Ensure that the planning process includes a clear definition of success: is it achieving the Plan or exceeding it? Is it being recognized by winning a certain award or by recruiting a particular team? How can individuals shine while the team excels?

- **Keep coming back to the Plan and the strategy.** You can never err by emphasizing the results anticipated in the Plan, clarifying the team's purpose, and leading the team to share knowledge, provoke thought, reflect, assess, and reassess. Prevent and dispel chaos by focusing the team on the future results that everyone wants to achieve.

- **Consider input from partners, both external and internal.**
  Just as no man is an island; neither should any team be one.
  Soliciting input as to how your team achieves its Plan from
  both inside and outside resources provides useful insights that
  you may not otherwise have considered. This includes input
  from your customers. But just as you must prevent your team
  from pursuing the wrong Plan, you must also be cautious
  about pursuing strategies that won't work for your unique
  team, regardless of advice to the contrary.

Consider this example:

To increase sales, a large fashion chain launches a wardrobe
advisory service as a marketing tool to help customers coordi-
nate their wardrobes. Because of the pressure from the marketing group in head office, Tom, the manager of a store
located in a rural area, works hard to rally around the initiative,
promoting the service to dubious team members and inviting
members of the marketing group to visit the store. As part of
the initiative, the marketing group representative implements
a plan whereby each customer is approached about the complimentary service. Unfortunately, not only is the store's clien-
tele turned off by the repeated requests to have their wardrobe
"reviewed," Tom's team does not have the opportunity to devise
a strategy that will work.

In this situation, Tom failed to balance the wishes of the head office
to have a uniform strategy with the unique characteristics of his market. In the short term, resisting the outright adoption of a corporate-
wide strategy is not always popular with those leading the initiative.
For example, there may be some egos attached to the new marketing
idea. Nevertheless, to lead the team to implement a strategy that is
flawed will hurt the team's results and diminish Tom's credibility in
the eyes of his team. Tom needed to spend time consulting with his
front-line staff who serve the customers. By combining their knowledge and experience with his enthusiastic engagement, Tom may have
achieved the sales results everyone wanted.

SUMMING UP

In an entrepreneurial situation, the opportunity to include team members is limited only by the owner's desire to do so, from granting equity positions to employees to setting the actual targets for the year. Aware that *involvement* is what really motivates people, many very successful entrepreneurs have reaped the benefits of asking employees to jump in with both feet and share their ideas as well as the resulting risks and rewards.

In a corporate setting, the requirements that end up being in various leaders' respective Plans are driven by the demands of shareholders, the chief executive officer, the finance group, and so on down the line. By the time a middle manager is told what he needs to deliver, there is minimal room for negotiation. However, don't think for a moment that your team is a victim and has no say in what it needs to do. In any management role in any size company, as the manager, you have a wonderful opportunity to engage your team by seeking out their ideas, expertise, and knowledge.

Chapter 13

INSPECT WHAT YOU EXPECT

Real Life

So you have involved everyone on the team in translating the Plan into an intelligent strategy and the team is on the road to achieving it. Or so you assume. No matter what strategy you have developed, you must still be prepared to continually assess and evaluate the results being achieved. *Inspect what you expect* is the not so subtle shorthand of the seasoned leader. Measuring individual and team performance in the short term, what is or is not being delivered this week, is the best way to build momentum and ensure results will be met over the longer term.

To keep track of short-term results, your personal presence and participation is required. Interpersonal relationships require presence; politicians know this well. Despite televised debates and virtual Web-based town hall meetings reaching millions of voters, success at the polls still requires knocking on doors, weaving through crowded rooms, kissing babies, and flipping burgers. What successful politicians and business leaders know is that there simply is no replacement for personal contact. Whether it is logical or not to do so, we primarily assess others, and are motivated by others, on the basis of our personal contacts with them.

Consider Kenneth A. Merchant's point of view from *Rewarding Results*, "Whereas periodic performance pressure stimulates creativity, consistent pressure is useful in a different way—it helps prevent sloppiness. Performance evaluations based on short measurement periods can be used to apply this desirable consistent performance pressure. Without pressure for short-term results, you'll just have people squander money."

With confident leadership (Responsibility 1), a team structure and process that captures competitive intelligence from inside and outside the organization and promotes team leadership (Responsibility 2), and the right strategy to achieve the Plan (Responsibility 3), you will be well-positioned to keep momentum focused on the attainment of required results in the short term.

MOBILIZING MOMENTUM

Your leadership role demands that you continually focus on the right things so that you can assess and evaluate events and results as they happen. This involves asking yourself the right questions:

- Are we on track to achieve the Plan, or off track?
- If off track, where and why?
- What needs to be done to get back on Plan?
- How much time do we have to do so?
- What are the critical risks?
- What obstacles are in the way?
- Who are the team members who can remove the obstacles so that the team can continue to stay or get on Plan?

- Do other people need to be involved in required changes? Does information need to be shared?
- If Plan A is not working, what's Plan B?

Decisions about marketing events, requests from head office, interpersonal conflicts, and underperformers on the team should all be considered from the perspective of what is most important for the *team* to be successful. When the leader has been diligent in understanding the Plan, and monitoring results, decisions of all kinds fall easily into place for the team.

FOLLOWING-UP

The need for most people to have a rapport and personal connection with a leader is illustrated by concepts such as management by walking around or the open-door policy, important approaches to consider if you want to be seen as a person and not an automaton closeted away in a corner office, or worse, as the sender of notes from a handheld electronic device! However, regular, well-planned one-on-one meetings are the essential link between the Plan and each member of the team, providing you the opportunity to first set specific goals and later to follow up on progress.

These meetings provide a way for you to personally continue to emphasize the link between the team's objectives with those of each individual, without over complicating things. Your team will not succeed because it has the best-looking performance plan documents on your personnel files. Your team's success will be determined by how well you are able to:

- *Listen to each team member* carefully to gain their individual insights, over and above what was shared in the group discussion.
- *Draw out the team member's concerns* and then act on what needs fixing, such as: administrative support, training in an area of key competency, more one-on-one time with you.
- *Agree on what needs to be accomplished*, the time frame in which it is to be done, benchmarks along the way, and

methods of carrying out the work. Following the meeting, send a note to the team members to set out what you understand was discussed and agreed. Ask yourself: Are my expectations clear? Are outcomes clear? Doing all this advance work eliminates the need to start from the ground floor with an underperforming individual. If a successful outcome has been properly envisioned by you and each team member, a gap between that outcome and the actual results is not only immediately obvious but the consequences are also understood, in a straightforward rather than threatening way.

- *Follow up on what is being done and not done* in whatever manner and time frame has been agreed upon, and do what needs to be done to get results on track. Don't balk at the follow-up; leadership is not rocket science and often success or failure rests not on the brilliance of a strategy but rather the persistence of the follow-up.

ON PLAN AND ON TARGET TO SUCCEED

In closing the discussion on the importance of understanding and implementing the Plan assigned to your team, we note that even with Plans that are not overly aggressive, and what seems to be a no-fail strategy, leaders can still fail. Why? Usually it is because they do not have the right people doing the right jobs. Perhaps they have recruited unwisely, assigned roles incorrectly, or lacked the courage to cut or move people as soon as it became clear they were underperforming. Or perhaps they missed the signs indicating that new "hot skills" were required to pull the team into the future. Too late, they realized that it is all about the people—and that is the subject of Responsibility 4: People.

SUMMING UP

Ultimately your performance will be measured to Plan in the short term. In the long term it will also be measured by your ability to consistently recruit the right team and help the individuals within it shine. Your star will rise with your ability to master the art of team building around a Plan and the depth of your interpersonal relationships with team members in getting there.

Do It Yourself!

Responsibility 3: The Plan

- **Know your Plan, know what matters.** No matter how well you and your team can do any other things, you need to achieve the Plan first, full stop.
- **Seek out guidance from your boss, successful peers, customers, and your team members to determine the team's real Plan.** Don't rush to judgment: what may appear to be your team's purpose may not in fact be true. Second-guess your first assumptions before charging down the wrong path.
- **Do everything possible to convey the importance of the nonnegotiables to your team.** Create reports and tracking methods that will keep everyone's focus on the right benchmarks.
- **Weigh requests against the impact on the Plan.** Whether it is a request for your individual time, your team's time and resources, or a special working arrangement for a team member, let your team know that requests are measured based on how they will affect the team's success.
- **Seek ways to accommodate special requests from team members (such as flexible work arrangements).** Once everyone knows your benchmark is the impact on the Plan, make people accountable for addressing that impact when they make special requests.
- **Involve the whole team in reviewing and understanding the Plan and building a viable strategy.** The more people participating, the greater their personal engagement.

- **Be wary of agreeing to strategies that don't seem to fit with your team's market.** Even if the head office is pressuring your team to participate, assess carefully whether it is a strategy that will be successful for your unique team.
- **Continually make personal connections with the team to ask positive questions about results.** Ask for and value the input and ideas of team members and look for ways to get out of your office and find out what is really happening.
- **Measure results in the short term.** The further out you push a consideration of results versus Plan, the greater the chance of getting irrevocably off Plan. Nothing can go too far off Plan if you measure, follow up, and set goals in the context of last week, this week, and next week.

RESPONSIBILITY 4

THE PEOPLE

*"People who feel good about themselves
produce good results..."*

Kenneth Blanchard,
Spencer Johnson,
The One Minute Manager

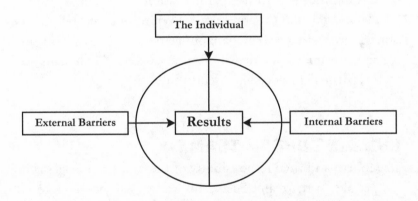

Real Life

To succeed as a team leader you must do two things:

1. In the short term, make sure that the team meets its Plan.
2. Over the long haul, lead a disciplined and principled team
    based on worthwhile values, made up of self-motivated
    people who get the job done.

> To accomplish these objectives, your leadership cannot be about command and control. And even having the best vision or the best ability to execute, isn't enough. To really succeed as a leader, you need to be able to bring top talent together and help the individuals do their best work. This requires astute recruitment and the creation of a culture that has energy and integrity.

We have discussed the first three responsibilities of a leader: (1) You, the leader, (2) the team structure, and (3) the Plan. These three responsibilities form the foundation for leading a team of people on a mission to get results. Woven throughout our discussion has been a singular emphasis on "getting it right" with the people on the team, so that they in turn can succeed. We'll focus now on this particular leadership opportunity.

BUILDING DREAM TEAMS

The fourth and final responsibility of the middle manager is for the people on the team. Successful leaders will be quick to tell you that their success is largely attributable to the great people on the team. Taking liberty with the premise of the *One Minute Manager*, people who feel great about themselves—because they believe they are an integral part of Plan achievement—produce great results, even in difficult circumstances, when they work on a great team.

Because next year's productivity targets will be higher than this year's targets, and so on into the future, we know that leading successfully once in a while or in the short term is not enough. Your role description calls for much more than achievement of this year's rote company performance indicators. In fact, in previous chapters we have noted that there are two performance indicators to focus on:

- The short-term achievement of the Plan
- The longer-term goal of managing a disciplined and principled workplace based on worthwhile values that are *personally important* to you and the rest of the team

It is only through success against the second performance indicator that you will be able to harness the full "intellectual property" and energy of the people you lead. And if you lead a young team, it is certainly true that many of those new talented recruits will be unwilling to work to their maximum potential if they do not "buy in" to the boss as a person worthy of their respect. Furthermore, they will seek out work in only those environments in which their insights and input are sought out and appreciated. Adding to the challenge, many young employees are "loners" by upbringing and may need assistance to develop the skill required to be an effective, collaborative team member.

IN PURSUIT OF PEOPLE SKILLS

Under this level of scrutiny, the so-called people skills required of a leader and all members of the team cannot be emphasized enough. Research conducted by Development Dimensions International Inc. asked 944 human resources professionals from 42 countries why leaders fail; 53 percent ranked "poor people skills" and "personal qualities" as the top two reasons. High on DDI's resulting list of "leadership potential indicators" were the ability to be "authentic," seen by the team as the genuine article, and the ability to bring out the best in people.

The exciting thing about a management role is that it allows you to choose an innovative approach in leading your team, regardless of its size or role. Even a small team can have a clear vision of the future and have members who are encouraged to make important decisions. Even a small team can take risks, be allowed to fail occasionally in so doing, consistently treat each other with respect, and encourage each other's progress and success.

SUMMING UP

Perhaps the most important principle in managing people is simply to stay on a path of respectful behavior—demonstrating respect for the organization's values goals and those of the people you lead. Consistency in being respectful in these ways is not always easy but is particularly influential on a new generation of future leaders who insist on working in environments where *mutual* respect and parity are paramount.

Finding ways to create a "dream team," one that "gels" and operates at optimal capacity, is your opportunity and privilege as a leader. It requires you to link together meaningful work for each individual with the goals of the whole team. If you can do this, you will earn the trust of those around you, people will want to work for you, and your team members will each have a strong sense of belonging, resulting in a willingness to go the extra mile. Undoubtedly, achieving these results provides the most significant intrinsic reward of being a leader.

Chapter 14

FULLY ENGAGING EVERY TEAM MEMBER

Real Life

The challenge of leading people is more art than science, requiring middle management to intelligently and effectively work with the external community beyond the team, to bring out the best in each individual on the team, and finally to lead a group of unique people—*as a team*—to optimal performance.

This is particularly difficult given the heightened expectations, the pace of change, and the sheer volume of communications we all are exposed to 24/7. Today's manager must help people cope with the distracting impact of numerous external influences on their ability to function within a team structure, so that the team cannot only perform, but perform at an optimal level, achieving the required results.

This requires an ability to rise above the daily minutiae to build and sustain relationships with all stakeholders that are based on reciprocity: ... a give-and-take that meets each individual stakeholder's needs. When a leader demonstrates this flexibility as well as an awareness of how various requests and demands affect results, it quickly becomes clear to everyone exactly what is achievable and negotiable and what is not.

GETTING DOWN TO BUSINESS

We know that productivity targets will likely increase again next year and the year after that. The challenge is how to achieve them without increasing the number of people on the team or burning the team out. Of course we want to "work smarter, not harder" within the structure of our defined Plan. To do so, particularly over the long term, the leader needs to ensure that the corporate values are shared with and by the team and the larger community.

DREAM LEADERS FOSTER INTUITIVE INTELLIGENCE

As we've discussed earlier, you have an opportunity to develop a culture within your team structure featuring a high degree of interpersonal communication with internal and external stakeholders. Your goal is to expand your team's community of supporters, including potential new employees, making recruitment a much easier task. This requires a unique intuitive intelligence on your part. Arupa Tesolin, an expert on intuitive intelligence in business, states, "Intuitive intelligence is *knowledge that arrives spontaneously*, beyond any known information or apparent thought process. Having a more intuitive workforce can add high value for the employer by anticipating solutions at early stages of a problem, improving client satisfaction, and even increasing workforce retention."

There are three types of intelligence: *instinctive* (a Canadian goose knows it must fly south); *intuitive* (complex problem solving on a subconscious level); and *sensory* (the ability to think logically and learn new facts). Most traditional business structures have been more comfortable with the use of logic and reasoning in the execution of business plans. This is, of course, still absolutely critical. However, team-based companies who are focused on increasing productivity recognize that the development and use of intuitive intelligence is critical to future success and growth.

So how is this achieved? Even when you have the right structures, processes, and plans in place leaders need to listen to their "gut" to manage interpersonal relationships. This comes from exposure to a variety of situations in life and in business, and from a personal authenticity.

In fact, intuitive leaders have the insight and confidence to provide team members with the opportunity for leadership too, within the context of Plan achievement. By providing opportunities for individuals to participate in the vision—a long-term rather than a short-term focus—and take responsibility for results, work takes on a greater meaning than a paycheck.

DREAM COMPANIES

In a 2005 Top Employers Survey of companies in the biopharmaceutical industry, the main characteristics used by employees to judge attractiveness of potential employer firms included the following six fundamental characteristics:

- Provides innovative leadership in its industry
- Presents a clear vision for the future
- Produces *important*, quality work
- Treats employees with respect
- Possesses loyal employees
- Provides a culture that aligns with individuals' personal values

This list provides good clues for leaders regarding the environment they create for their employees. You personally can choose to take an innovative leadership approach in leading your team, regardless of its size or role, and by doing so, meet the expectations in the workplace today of the "dream leader in a dream company."

A REALISTIC VIEW TO BUILDING COMMUNITY

Without people, there are no leadership roles, there are no team structures or processes required, and quite frankly, no Plan would be achievable. These facts should always serve to put the leader's role into a humbling perspective. As any team coach will tell you, working with individuals can be challenging, and working with individuals toward a team effort can be exasperating. However, people management can also be the greatest source of satisfaction for the professional manager who understands, as a starting point, a basic principle: *leadership is a job at which you can't be perfect.*

A leader who believes that she will "get it right" every time—some day—is seeking perfection in a job where success, however it is quantified, is fleeting. The reality is that before the winning team has even received the silver platter from the head office, the senior engineer has moved to a competitor, a new business plan has been handed out, and the software system is being entirely revamped. In moments of fatigue, a dispirited leader may ask himself, "It's always about what have you done for me lately? I just can't seem to win." You need to be realistic and accept that building a team is ongoing, cumulative, and neverending. To do your best work, understand that you preside over a continuous work in progress.

As a leader, it is necessary to step back from the fray and in an organized and systematic way to do two things:

- Bring together the needs and interests of the people on your team with those of others, both in the company and in the community.
- Engage each individual to participate to their optimal performance level.

Some Personal Insights on Perfectionism

Perfectionism is a burden. Those who suffer from it act out of a fear of failure. One could even go so far as to say they are egotistical in that they think that it is possible for humans to strive to a state of perfection in every action they take. This is, of course, impossible. So perfectionists are never free of their burden. Never content with who they are, they are notoriously difficult to work for. There is a difference between setting the bar high to strive for excellence, and the self-sabotaging behaviors surrounding perfectionism. Remember, as Dr. Ross Lawford, author of *The Quest for Authentic Power*, says, "you are... enough." When it feels like there is no fun left in your job, relax a bit, and try to take it easier on yourself and others.

SUMMING UP

Because of corporate realities today, a group of individuals working independently can no longer match the effectiveness of a strong and cohesive team. To achieve ever more onerous productivity targets, your focus must be on managing the individuals you lead within the context of overall team success at achieving its Plan.

Chapter 15

MAKE A DIFFERENCE
AND A PROFIT

Real Life

As we have discussed, a key challenge for management at every level today is increased productivity, and while it is relatively straightforward for a finance group or chief accountant to calculate the cost of earning a dollar of revenue, it is much more difficult to measure whether your employee salary and benefits expense is really getting maximum results for the money spent. One thing is certain: if you are unable to motivate individuals to work at their maximum capacity, you cannot hope to succeed in today's challenging domestic and global economy.

To increase productivity, the leader must increase the personal motivation of the people on the team. And although monetary compensation is very important to most people, money alone does not ensure a highly motivated team. Highly motivated people, in fact, are *self-motivated;* accordingly, your role is to provide an environment most conducive to moving people in that direction.

SELF-MOTIVATION

Work cultures that are likely to inspire a high degree of self-motivation in team members often provide:

- Vision and Inspiration: understanding and believing in where the team is headed
- Opportunity: the personal ability to play a key role in developing the team's vision and ultimate success
- Understanding: What? Why? How?
- Execution Guidelines: values and priorities in meeting expectations
- Preparedness: ability to practice and increase skills to maximize energy
- Recognition: from peers and superiors
- Evaluation: within an open, nonthreatening environment

In essence, to really engage people, a leader must quite simply give people good work to do and a chance to do it really well in the right environment.

Any good teacher will tell you that to be effective, motivating, and memorable, you have to "get into your students' heads," find out what turns them on, and then help them not only to pass the grade but to excel in developing their areas of talent. Most of us can recall a teacher or mentor who made a difference in our lives—who caused us to think about things in a different way, supported us through a difficult time, or brought us an "ah-ha" moment or two.

Effectiveness at this level requires leaders to find ways to engage the *whole brain*: to secure commitment from individuals *to take risks*, removing themselves from their comfort zones and going confidently forward to the next level in their ability to perform. *Individual and team engagement is usually only found when management has sent a clear message that the occasional failure is both inevitable and acceptable: opportunities to learn, not point fingers.*

Self-motivated people also need opportunities to practice their skills and take on new challenges so that work becomes a *continuum of achievement,* a requirement for enthusiastic engagement. In most organizations, the opportunity to present your team members with new personal challenges exists every day, particularly if those in management keep attuned to how important this is in ensuring high motivation. No matter how good we are today, leaders who allow their teams to continuously practice on new terrain create a nimble culture most likely to be highly productive over the long term.

MASTERFUL PERFORMANCES

Consider the example of Newmont—the largest gold company in the world which started close to 100 years ago in 1921. The statement of their vision and values tells a succinct story of sustained excellence underlying their ability to prosper over a century of dramatic change. In their mission statement they vow to:

- Act with integrity, trust, and respect
- Reward an entrepreneurial spirit, a determination to excel and a commitment to action
- Demand leadership in safety, stewardship of the environment, and social responsibility
- Develop the best people in pursuit of excellence
- Insist on teamwork and honest communication
- Demand positive change by continually seeking out and applying best practices

The foundations for consistent, winning performance in times of constant change are clear:

- **Set a vision for excellence.** It takes just as much energy to think big as it does to think small . . . so think big and challenge your team and each individual on it to do the same.
- **Recruit top performers.** Employ people who have the right attitudes as well as the right skill sets.
- **Provide a nonthreatening environment** in which employees can work to their full potential and receive rewards that

matter to them, including the pride of individual achievement and the chance to be part of a winning team.

THE PROBLEM WITH PERFORMANCE REVIEWS

The intention behind performance reviews is good: to help people develop their strengths and minimize their weaknesses. But in our experience, a couple of timeworn people management tools are not especially useful in working with self-motivated people. One such tool is the "performance review" and another is an inflexible "incentive" program.

The performance review is sometimes viewed as an annual event, most notable for the anxiety it creates and its amazing ability to negatively affect a "buzz" of productive behavior. Worse, it is often used as an excuse for not providing ongoing feedback on an individual's activities and results. Unfortunately, many companies have performance review programs embedded in complicated policies, causing some managers to avoid what they see as a regimented (and difficult) process. If this is true for *you*, you need to break free of the cumbersome rules around the review process and move to developing one-on-one rapport with each team member through whatever plan that works for you and the team member. Keep in mind that *substance over process* is key in establishing meaningful performance dialogues.

Similarly, performance incentive plans are often intractably in place in large companies. The wise leader recognizes that such plans can never have the built-in flexibility required to cover all the situations meriting recognition or reward or both. To the degree that you have the flexibility and budget to do so, gifts of new "valuations"—time or health or family-oriented rewards—can often make a significant difference to your employees.

Here is an example:

Margie is a top performer in her team. Her manager, Bryan, knows that she values time with her new grandchild. She has recently prepared an innovative new template for an administrative procedure.

The Wrong Move. Bryan fails to acknowledge the work or talks about the team's new efficiency without acknowledging Margie's contributions, or even worse, accepts your boss's kudos without mentioning Margie's role.

The Consequence. Margie is turned off, feels she has no impact, and stops using innovation for the improvement of results. Meanwhile, Margie looks for the next opportunity to move positions, decreasing her potential productivity and quite possibly also influencing the rest of the team.

The Right Move. Bryan recognizes Margie's individual achievement immediately by becoming interested in the steps to delivery or execution of Margie's innovation while it is a work in progress (asking how and why questions to "get into Margie's brain"); asks Margie to report on the innovation at team meetings; celebrates the achievement within the team; and, if resources allow, gives Margie unexpected time off to visit with her grandchild.

The Consequence: Margie has experienced the happiness that comes from setting her own goals, controlling the work and how she does it, being recognized for her efforts, and a bonus of time—much more valuable than money for this employee.

A final thought about personal motivation: when people are given the ability to help others, especially when they have the opportunity to rally around a great cause, such as raising money to help a seriously ill child get advanced medical treatment, something wonderful happens: people become more generous with their time, thoughts, and money. Those same generous people do not change when they walk into work; most people want to be good people in all arenas of their lives. A leader who can engage people to have a direct impact on the team's results positively influences employee effectiveness and productivity. Find a way to help your people contribute to the team with distinction and pride.

SUMMING UP

Tom Brokaw, the former news anchor, said: "It's easy to make a buck... it's a lot tougher to make a difference." The leader who can make people feel that they *are* making a difference takes employee productivity to a whole new level.

Chapter 16

A CLASS ACT TO FOLLOW

> ### Real Life
>
> Prospective employees ask questions about it; our team members refer to it when mentioning their work to the next door neighbor; it can enhance the bottom line or be the cause of protracted and bitter litigation. What is this "it"?
>
> It is the culture of your team: that amorphous quality that cannot be pinned to one event, action, word, or person but pervades and influences every aspect of the teams we lead. Your team's culture is *up to you.*
>
> Does your team have the "buzz"? Is yours the team people are clamoring to work on? What does it take to have the team that not only meets expectations consistently, but exceeds them—and has a great time doing so?
>
> Wouldn't everyone love to work for a team like that?

Most people spend more time at work than with their family or partners. They often invest more hours into the company's Plan than their own life plan, often at the expense of their personal relationships, let alone preferred leisure activities such as golf, fishing, or adhering to a workout schedule. It is amazing how much people will give up to get their work done, something that a manager should never take for granted. The astute manager should ask himself, is Mark sending e-mails until midnight because he is particularly engaged in project X right now, or is it at the ongoing expense of quality time with his partner or other key stakeholders in his personal life?

A wise manager will be very careful about nurturing balance in the lives of people on the team. That manager will be the first to think about the impact of work on health and family, and respectful of pressing deadline demands on personal lives. Done right, leadership that sparks efficiency, high performance, and team momentum *improves* overall life quality of team members. Top managers make that happen.

It is astounding how much a leader's personality, values, habits, and even lifestyle influence the team. An article by Jim Gray in the *National Post*, entitled "Managing People with Class and Grace," made the point that ". . . class carries with it more authority than ever before because it is such a rare commodity." The article went on to suggest that commonplace habits such as using e-mail to avoid difficult conversations or leaving an event early without saying good-bye to all tablemates or the hosts are indicative of the "low-class" behavior that can diminish a leader's authority.

IT'S ABOUT THE CULTURE

Linda Duxbury, a professor at the Sprott School of Business at Carleton University, conducted a research study of a hundred companies. Her research indicated that most companies do not succeed at developing a corporate culture that values treating people respectfully, with all that "respect" includes: appropriate language and behavior, an appreciation of good work done, and leaders who demonstrate emotional maturity in how they handle both the good and bad daily occurrences.

There's little doubt that most companies today have written policies outlining in careful detail the guiding principles held by senior leadership, likely drafted with the help of experienced human resources professionals and legal advisers. However, in any company with more than one team (most companies!), those principles come alive for individuals only if their most immediate leader (and often his or her leader) is committed to the ideas and values espoused by the written policies. In fact, for an organization to have company-wide adherence to the policies, three things need to be in place:

- A chief executive officer who "walks the talk"
- A commitment by the CEO to hire leaders who emulate his or her beliefs in the importance of a respectful workplace
- A method of measuring and rewarding adherence to the written policies, in the same way that financial results are measured and rewarded

However, there is no need to wait for those factors to be in place in your company. Your immediate opportunity is entirely within your own control, through your own behavior with your team. It is in this realm that leadership really requires you to set the tone and accordingly, you can set whatever tone you like or need.

LIKING THE BOSS

A total of 68 percent of the 9,655 respondents to a 2005 survey on the online job site Monster.com said that liking their boss made it much easier to love their job, and 15 percent said they actually choose a job based on their personality fit with their boss. While there is an important difference between being your team's friend and being approachable, fair, and friendly, team members who acknowledge "liking" their boss and therefore "loving" their jobs, will be heavily influenced by the way that leader goes about setting the tone for the team and creating the culture of the workplace.

It would be naïve to think that every team should or could be identical in its culture. The successful team leader in investment banking will impart hard-working drive and determination, and focus less on diplomacy and tact than would be required in a head office team creating new products. *The point simply is that every team functions most effectively where individuals are equally respected and recognized;* the leader is primarily responsible for creating and sustaining that culture, even when new people join the team or it goes through a corporate reorganization.

SETTING EXPECTATIONS

The ground rules about what is and isn't acceptable in the team culture are almost entirely achieved through modeling desired behavior, not publishing rules and guidelines. Examples of the types of expectations best conveyed through your own behavior are itemized below:

- **Equal recognition.** Valuing each person's contribution equally, whether in a complex, highly compensated role or a more administrative position is essential.
- **Consistently pleasant disposition.** First and foremost: smiling more and having a sense of humor. One of our colleagues shared with us his personal theory on the "two camps" of people in the world: the smilers and the nonsmilers. Be a smiler.
- **Proactive problem solving.** Raising problems rather than covering them up or only focusing on the positives.
- **Innovation encouraged.** Seeking innovative solutions to problems and thinking of creative approaches; this, of course, requires an open mind and an egoless approach to new ideas that are linked to the Plan.
- **Astute forgiveness.** Viewing problems and crises as opportunities to learn something for next time, together with the ability to capture mistakes and communicate within new policies and procedures, so that other team members can learn and avoid them.
- **Authentic and infectious enthusiasm.** Demonstrating excitement about good things that happen, whether to a team member in her personal life, or to the team in terms of exceeding its sales target or winning an award. Give your team permission to cut loose and celebrate once in a while—the smiles and high fives are infectious.

Some Personal Insights on Working Hard, Playing Hard

Many high achievers are known to embrace a "work hard, play hard" attitude. If you are one of them, showing up on time with the goods to take on the day with gusto is not negotiable, even if you were out too late the night before. Time management is critical; no point knowing it all if you don't show up on time for the exam. Remember what your parents sternly said the next day: set the alarm, pull your act together, and don't show up disheveled. Go the extra mile—show up well-dressed and leave time for coffee and breakfast. Do it on time, every time.

CELEBRATING EXCELLENCE

The list could go on, of course, but the last point we mention—celebrating excellence—should not be difficult in a workplace. Yet, remarkably, people can be slow to recognize achievement or give positive feedback, even to those with whom they are close. Ask any mother how appreciated she feels, day after day, and you'll understand immediately. *Pride in being part of a winning team should be encouraged and demonstrated as a valued principle.*

Imagine if the team members of the Edmonton Oilers or the LA Kings hockey teams had failed to celebrate the greatness of The Great One, Wayne Gretzky, because they felt threatened by his incredible skill. Not only would they have failed to embrace the opportunity to reach a new level of individual and team excellence by observing and playing with the greatest hockey player on earth, they would have lost the obvious personal opportunity in being part of the buzz that followed Gretzky everywhere in his hockey career.

It is also easy to forget the team's consistent, reliable performers, and begin to take those who support us best on the team for granted, particularly when most of your day is spent firefighting.

Instead, we place these wonderful people too often into a box, labeled "Whew, No Problem," as a coping mechanism in dealing with those team members who are demanding and tend to wear us out. This is dangerous. When 80 percent of your time is spent on the distracters, the team will suffer, losing productivity and often its best people to the competition.

APPRECIATING YOUR TEAM EVERY DAY

The point is that your expectations about the "softer" side of the team culture are conveyed, one way or another, for good or bad, every day. It is easy to demonstrate leadership when things are going well. Acting with grace and dignity during difficulties is not so easy. Nevertheless, no matter the level of your leadership role, if you are responsible for a team, it is up to you to create a respectful, energetic work environment and not wait for corporate policies or the actions of the chief executive officer to do that for you. *Neither written policies nor the CEO are as influential as you when it comes to your team wanting to go into work every day.*

AVOIDING AND MANAGING CONFLICT

People are different. That's what makes management so challenging... and interesting. Conflict can sneak up on you in a variety of ways: passively, secretively, or "in your face." You need to be aware of it, prevent it if you can, and above all else, deal with it.

One dictionary defines conflict as a state of open, often prolonged, fighting; a battle or war. While this does not seem conducive to creating a respectful workplace, some have suggested to us that "a little conflict" is a good thing, bringing in new ideas and forcing people to think clearly about issues.

We believe this perspective confuses conflict itself with just one aspect of conflict, namely, substantive differences of opinion. Differences of opinion are normal and healthy in a team, but to become a conflict a divisive emotional element needs to be added (leading to the dictionary's usage of words like *battle* and *war*). This destructive element has no place in a constructive and respectful workplace.

Incidences of employee absences for work-related stress have risen steadily over the past decade. In a recent survey conducted by the Chartered Institute of Personnel and Development (CIPD), almost 40 percent of employers reported an increase in stress-related leave. Preventing and managing conflict as a leader is an essential component of minimizing the negative impact caused to team productivity by stress, whether as a result of interpersonal conflicts or inappropriate behavior by individuals on the team.

Certain conflict-causing behaviors that we have listed below simply cannot be tolerated—period. When they occur, they must be addressed immediately or the individual, the team, and possibly the company will risk serious damage to productivity.

We agree that every individual on a team should be encouraged to regularly share his thoughts and ideas, and the value of those ideas largely rests on their uniqueness and the possibility that they are different from those of the colleague in the next chair. However, too often, fighting and dissension in a team go beyond a reasoned debate on an issue and yet are benignly viewed as constructive conflict. The leader's role is to manage his or her behavior, the behavior of team members, and the processes of the team in such a way as to minimize conflict while encouraging reasoned and reasonable debate on ideas and issues, and avoiding dissension and acrimony. In our experience, conflict left unchecked creates the antithesis of a respectful workplace and is one of the most obvious negative links between the team environment and team success.

IDEAS TO CONSIDER IN MANAGING CONFLICT

- **Your behavior is key.** If you are slow to provoke and demonstrate an openness to feedback and new ideas, most team members will follow suit. A leader who herself provokes heated discussions in team meetings and is regularly engaged in "warfare" with other departments, clients, or head office signals that an aggressive conflict style of work behavior is appropriate.

- **Consider your approach to conflict if and when it arises.** Often the best approach is to encourage team members in conflict to work through the dispute themselves, thereby clarifying that you do not see your role to be that of an arbitrator of interpersonal conflict. While this will work in those cases where both parties are mature and interested in resolving their differences, in some cases, you will find a member of your team in successive conflicts with different people, leading to our next point.

- **Some individual team members may need to leave the team.** If that sounds harsh, we are not suggesting that their departure would be your first attempted solution. Clearly there is a chance that an individual has an episode or two of conflict in the team and can be encouraged to practice a new style, at least while in the team. However, it is our experience that those people who engage in the most disruptive conflict do not do so accidentally or even occasionally; rather it is an integral part of their personality and has no role in a cohesive team.

- **Address procedures.** Delegating who does what and when will assist in minimizing the times when conflict appears to be the only alternative.

- **Increase communication at times of change.** This will work to reduce conflict created by uncertainty about the future, especially during times of corporate merger or acquisition.

- **Consider working with a member of your human resources group or an outside consultant.** Perhaps take the team through one of the many "personal style" evaluations that are available. Quite often an accurate, insightful, and well-managed evaluative process can illuminate why disagreements are occurring. If one person in a close working relationship is oriented entirely to getting results and the other individual prefers to establish harmonious personal relationships above all else, there will be at best a certain amount of impatience on one hand and hurt feelings on the

other, and at worst, a complete unwillingness to coopera-
tively work together. With an awareness of what is really
behind their respective differences, many people can successfully accommodate what they see as their colleagues' idiosyncrasies.

UNDERSTANDING ANGER

Managing conflict also requires an understanding of what makes
people angry, which is most often when they perceive they have
been treated unfairly or an injustice has taken place. A manager
cannot possibly address every perceived slight, but some offending
behaviors must be dealt with immediately.

Today's intuitive leaders put behaviors that lead to conflict into
two groups: negotiables and nonnegotiables. Negotiables are cor-
rectable with awareness and explanation, together with a clear
expectation that the offending behavior will cease. Nonnegotiables
will not be tolerated and will lead to dismissal, either immediately
or following appropriate notice that did not result in the required
changes. It is wise to construct a list of conflict-causing behaviors
for discussion with your team and each new individual to join it,
in consultation with your human resource department.

Conflict-Causing Behaviors

The Negotiables	The Nonnegotiables
Failure to listen	Bullying
Generalizations	Harassment
Power-based communication	Bullying and unscrupulous behavior to "get ahead" in the company
Me-based communication	Twisting stories, blaming others

Inappropriate reassurances	Innuendo
Defensiveness	Aggressiveness
Overstatement	Need to control
Use of absolute words or statements	Unreliable, frequent tardiness
Ignorance of cultural differences	Lying, stealing, or any other unethical behaviors
Taking credit	Discrimination

MANAGING CRISES

The strength of a relationship is really defined by what happens when times are tough. "In sickness and in health"—those words echoed by so many couples in their marriage vows define the commitment to a relationship in good times and in bad. All relationships suffer periods of instability and many relationships also experience times of crisis.

Surviving negative changes in relationships usually means that the relationship had a firm footing before the crisis, and that both parties demonstrated maturity throughout the difficult period. This is true in the workplace as well. If you make a practice of consistently showing and expecting respect, honesty, fairness, and responsibility, your words and actions in a crisis will carry significant weight.

Tips of Managing Crisis

1. When your team's reputation has taken a hit due to a significant failure of process, such as leaked confidential information, a product recall, or a scandal, you must be open and honest.
2. Disclose as much information as possible to minimize uninformed gossip.

3. Display the highest ethical behavior in your actions.
4. Make it right.

Source: From the 2005 Top Employer's Survey,
Peter Gwynne, scienceCareers.org.

Times of great change can become crises if they are mishandled. The most obvious examples occur during mergers or acquisitions, or when a leader comes or goes. At these times, personnel crises are most often the result of either a failure to communicate fully or disrespectful termination procedures that can cause productive teams to stop functioning completely.

Regardless of the reason for a crisis, or the level of a manager, everyone responsible for leading people can have significant influence on how those people react to the situation. We have heard employees say that even hearing, "I can't tell you everything I am told, but I commit to telling you as much as I can," somewhat alleviates the feeling of having no control. In short, successful recovery depends on the integrity you have always shown, combined with doing the right thing when the crisis occurs, reassuring the team that, with time, "this, too, shall pass."

SUMMING UP

There is no aspect of leadership in which you are more personally influential than in creating the team culture: imparting a caring and enthusiastic team spirit can only be done through an investment of your own personality, humor, and focus.

Chapter 17

COOKIE-CUTTER COACHING
WORKS FOR COOKIES

Real Life

In years gone by, coaching meant leading a sports team. More recently, the word has been adopted by business to include everything from outside consultants working one-on-one with executives to enhance their performance, to companywide initiatives intended to impart consistency, to employee-manager discussions throughout the enterprise. In short, coaching has become the trendy thing to do in the workplace and far be it from any manager to claim that he doesn't coach his team members. Your challenge is to find a way to make coaching part of what you do and who you are, rather than a tedious add-on task to your already full schedule.

WHAT KIND OF MENTOR ARE YOU?

We're all better in the warm comfort of our personal mentor. This person may be your spouse, parent, teacher, boss, or any other trusted advisor, who knows you well enough and cares about you enough to tell it like it is, every time. Those of us who have such a person in our lives are much better for it. If we are lucky enough to have a boss who helps us reach our potential—even if that means hearing some things we would rather not hear—it's a very good thing. *Are you that kind of boss?*

The extent to which companies have bought into coaching as worthy of their time and money is seen in the experience of the Human Resources Professionals Association of Ontario. In 2003, only three requests for advice on companywide coaching were received; in 2004, there were 18. In 2005, however, the volume of requests led the Association to organize a conference on the topic which was attended by 77 for-profit companies and 12 from the public sector.

The positive aspect of all this attention to coaching is its reinforcement to leaders of the benefits of *talking* to the people in the team in a generally constructive and problem-solving way. The downside is that by labeling any activity, we tend to view it as more complicated or difficult than it necessarily needs to be, and so we may shy away from doing it at all.

In the best coaching situations, the education goes both ways. Examples abound of top executives whose success is largely attributed to finding many opportunities to engage in a conversation with people at all levels and in all places in the company, coming away far more enlightened about what the company is doing right or wrong. And, of course, those with whom the CEO spoke— whether they are on an assembly line or serving up milkshakes—will have gained a better understanding of what keeps the big boss up at night. One would hope that if these CEOs were advised that they were engaging in the activity labeled *coaching* that they wouldn't shy away from doing it for fear of getting it wrong.

We encourage you to think of coaching as a central part of your job that should be as natural as dealing with the inflow of e-mails. We've all known managers who stayed all day in their offices, facing the computer, leading people to ask each other, "What does she do all day?" The simple fact is that the best way to coach people is to "be there." Don't stay locked in the corner office. Err on the side of visibility. If you can, get out on the floor, and take the time to stop every day at different desks or offices or throughout the assembly line to meet and greet those who perform with you and for you. This is an invaluable, respectful courtesy that will pay off in spades for you when the going gets tough. Ask questions in the positive:

- What successes did you have today?
- Are you getting the results you want?
- Is there anything new that is especially encouraging to you?

DON'T MICROMANAGE; MICROENCOURAGE

Resist the temptation to micromanage or to be drawn into a negative or technical conversation (say, "Why don't we discuss that at our weekly meeting?"). Instead, touch people with your sincere interest in their day-to-day achievements and how they are contributing positively toward the Plan. While discouragement comes from indifference and rejection, recognition and encouragement are the keys to better performance.

Keep in mind the basic marketing fundamental: to be effective, a marketing message must be repeated six or seven times to drive buying behavior; likewise, stopping to encourage people in the workplace needs to happen often and regularly.

Scheduled one-on-one meetings are also part of being a coach; these are in addition to the informal chats. The format of these planned meetings needs to be as varied as the number of people on your team. Numerous books and articles have been written setting out checklists of 21 questions to ask yourself after a coaching session; the four areas you will need to develop within yourself before you can coach; and the five basic questioning techniques to use as a coach. All of this advice may be an excellent resource for certain coaching situations or certain leadership personalities, but these suggestions cannot possibly factor in the unique people that you lead and their particular needs.

BALL GAMES, HOT DOGS, AND BEER

Over a beer and a hotdog at a ball game may be the best place to subtly coach a high-potential person who is hoping for a major promotion soon. A formal meeting to discuss his premature aspirations may simply be embarrassing to him. On the other hand, a team member who is not delivering the required results will likely best be served by a private, lengthy meeting, well-planned by you in advance, during which you can outline the situation as you see it, ask for his or her input and feedback, and work together to agree on what needs to be done next by each of you.

The point is that ongoing dialogue attuned to each team member is essential and should not be set aside for a rainy day because you believe that the coaching process is difficult, boring, repetitious, or a nice-to-do rather than a need-to-do. Our experience is that in engaging regularly with each member of your team, you need to cover (in your mind, if not on paper) the four points listed in the next sidebar.

Tips for Engaging Individuals

1. **Personal rapport**. Develop or maintain personal rapport as a foundation for future positive or negative situations that arise.
2. **Know their current work objectives**. Ensuring required individual objectives are being met is easier when you know what they are; ask and follow up.
3. **Know their career objectives**. Understand and respond to his or her career aspirations and manage expectations around those aspirations honestly and appropriately.
4. **Ask for advice**. Seek input and guidance on the team's direction, client feedback, challenges, and opportunities for the team, and what you as the leader can be doing better. Then put suggestions into actions and acknowledge the contribution.

FORMAL IN-OFFICE MEETINGS

A formal meeting schedule for coaching works best in these two situations:

1. At the outset of a working relationship, for example, if you are a new leader or if you have recruited a new person
2. Where individual objectives are not being met

In either case, setting up weekly meetings enables you to be sure that (a) the meeting occurs, and (b) all relevant discussion items can be covered and ideally documented, with a brief follow-up note from you after the meeting confirming what was discussed.

In coaching situations where objectives are not being met, two principles are particularly important:

1. **The first principle is to separate the person from the results.** This is essential both in your own mind going into the meeting and verbally to the person. No matter the level of your disappointment with the results, the results are separate from the person. The *person* will likely have contributed to the team in the past (or is doing so now, just not in all areas). Even if that is not the case—the results are not there now and never have been—remember as you begin a discussion with him that like you, he is a Dad, a spouse, a baseball coach, a volunteer, a worthy person who will go home to his family that evening just as you will. A leader's long-term objectives have never once been achieved by diminishing a person's self-worth.
2. **The second principle has been coined by Stephen Covey as "letting arguments fly out open windows."** An individual who makes accusations or loses his cool in an explosion of hurtful words and expletives during a meeting with you is where your leadership mettle is tested. You simply must let it go. Think of your emotional team member as grasping onto a length of string, one end of which he tosses at you with his angry words. The temptation is to pick up

your end of the string by retorting in kind, perhaps with a defensive answer or your own accusation. Resist this temptation and focus on how you want the meeting to end: on a calmer note with you not having made statements that you are already regretting.

The one thing that you can be sure of is that your comments made in anger or frustration to a team member will be repeated to at least one other person, and rarely in those repeated stories will she mention the ill-considered words that he or spoke!

SUMMING UP

The essence of coaching is a two-way dialogue from which both parties come away having learned something. You will get better results with coaching—and enjoy the process much more—if you do away with the traditional idea that the person being coached has more to learn than the coach. One of the greatest benefits from your coaching sessions, formal or informal, will be the knowledge that *you* gain from the discussions.

Chapter 18

DO YOU LIKE HIM? LISTEN TO YOUR INNER VOICE WHEN YOU HIRE

Real Life

It is naïve to think that a plethora of interviewing techniques and testing are the panacea for hiring the best people available. Every manager can regale you with stories of how the perfect candidate for a job, carefully interviewed and double-checked, turned out to be a complete failure. Sometimes it is a cultural issue: the new recruit simply doesn't fit in with the rest of the team. This is a hard nuance to discern in advance of the first week or month on the job. Other times the individual's technical experience does not meet the expected level.

Regardless of the reason, a certain percentage of job hires made by hiring managers prove to be mistakes. With this in mind, you need to go above and beyond the standard tests and processes and rely on some good old-fashioned common sense when it comes to hiring: listening to your intuition and taking the necessary time to get the very best people on your team.

IT BOILS DOWN TO YOUR GUT

There are an abundance of tools, tests, and techniques to assist managers in recruitment. These tools may be useful in sorting through a number of candidates in a systematic and uniform manner. Many of the tests that are available to assess candidates' personalities, skills, and aptitudes are often very predictive, offering a useful baseline for hiring decisions and a framework for working with the chosen candidate after he or she has joined the team. However, in light of the high rate of hiring failure, you need to keep in mind some commonsense points about recruitment which are sometimes overlooked.

Don't Delegate Recruitment

Leaders of the best teams tend to get heavily involved in recruitment for every position, never relinquishing this participation in recruiting for key roles. The involvement of the top person in a small company may not be able to continue indefinitely as the company expands, but the point is that it is hard to think of a more important job for a leader than recruiting people who fit the team culture and share the leader's values.

Don't Dismiss Your Intuition

This bears repeating: we may assume that since this is a business, not a personal relationship, we should downplay the small voice that says "I don't really *like* that person." There is a good chance that your intuition is telling you something valuable based on your experience. That your unconscious mind is uneasy is indeed an important message to consider and test out by having the candidate meet others in the company whose opinion you respect and also by having further meetings, perhaps in a social setting, where you may be better able to assess the source of your discomfort and whether it is valuable feedback to consider.

Listen More Than You Talk

Why do we focus so much on the right *questions* to ask? A whole lot more information from and about a candidate can be gleaned by listening carefully to the reply to *any* question, and yet too often interviewers use an interview to expound at length on themselves and the company. Instead, focus on listening not only to the substance of the replies but also the nature of them.

Tips on Interviewing and Hiring

- Is the candidate longwinded and rambling?
- Is the answer on point?
- Does the candidate recognize that conversation, even an interview, is a lobbing of a ball back and forth between two people or does he or she expound at length without coming up for air?
- Does the candidate allow you to clarify or confirm points?
- Is the tone of the responses predominantly negative or positive; in other words, does the interviewee speak disparagingly about past or current employers or other relevant parties such as industry regulators, suppliers, or clients?

Looked at from this perspective, the questions you ask can be lofty and important, such as how they exercise leadership skills in their life, or about their son's hockey team. Often any question, listened to carefully, will reveal important clues about the candidate's character and personality. Here are some additional suggestions for successful hirings:

- **Check references and ask to speak with nonreferences who have worked with the person.** Make up a response template to capture the anecdotal comments of the people you call and determine a trend line.
- **Ask colleagues to meet the person but don't expect a rubber stamp.** Often a leader will be set on hiring a person and yet will ask colleagues to meet him "as a final step." The fact is, contrary opinions are often unwelcome at that point: someone in the company has already become fully engaged in bringing the candidate on board. If that is the case, don't

waste colleagues' time by seeking their opinion but you may wish to ask yourself whether you have done justice to this recruitment by perhaps short-circuiting the process.

- **Ask a top performer in the role to interview the person.** Often no one can sense who will be good in a role better than a person already performing well in that capacity. With the insight that actually doing the job brings, the top performer can sometimes flush out inconsistencies and insincerity in a candidate's responses. The only caution is to think through the dynamics of having an interview done by someone who will be the peer of the new hire; if the meeting is informal and perhaps in a social setting, this may not be a concern, but an actual "interview" in such a situation may result in the working relationship starting off on an awkward footing.

SUMMING UP

Mistakes in hiring are costly. Not only can they cost you money in severance packages, they cause your team to lose valuable time and the momentum needed to achieve its Plan. Your company's reputation in the marketplace is also negatively affected every time you make a mistake and bring on the wrong person. In the important process of recruitment, keep your eyes open and don't get caught up in situations where the outcome (hire Smith) is prematurely a foregone conclusion. You need to take the time to do this well.

Do It Yourself!

Responsibility 4: The People

- **Engage your team members.** Choose recruits who can be as involved as possible in setting the vision for the team and making sure they have the opportunity (and responsibility) to play a key role in achieving the vision. This requires an ability to focus on the future, something you should look for when interviewing.

- **Recognize daily.** Keep in mind that the best performance reviews occur every day as you take the time to notice what your team members are doing right. Recognize their achievements, privately and publicly.
- **Be personal with incentives.** Look for ways within your available structure and budget to provide incentives and rewards that are personally motivating for the people you lead.
- **Set the right tone.** Be a class act and set a respectful yet good humored tone to your team environment. Lead the way in having the people on the team appreciate the contributions made by their peers. Create an environment where excellence is celebrated while still being open about problems and issues as they arise.
- **Ask yourself** if your own habits and behaviors are congruent with a respectful and vibrant workplace. Stretch yourself and make the changes you know are needed.
- **Manage conflict.** Realize the damage that can be done by emotional and personal dissension. Never let healthy discussions become acrimonious disputes; dealing with offenders promptly is your job as a manager.
- **Coach creatively.** Finding the right time, place, and approach in coaching team members is essential. View coaching as simply finding the best way to develop and maintain a strong relationship with the people on your team, one which will let you "tell it like it is" when necessary.
- **Take your time to recruit the best people.** Consider bringing on new people at pivotal times in your team's development. Know whether you want to maintain, change, or improve your team culture. Don't underestimate the value of your intuition in assessing how a person will positively or negatively impact your existing team. Finding the right new team member entails far more than filling a job description.

PART 2

GETTING RESULTS FROM RESPONSIBLE LEADERSHIP

OPPORTUNITY 1

TAKING TIME FOR ASSESSMENT AND EVALUATION

Real Life

It's Monday morning—the start of another action-packed week. Are we ready to achieve the results we want? Does the team know what projects it will complete and which will begin? Are the individuals on the team poised to reach their goals? This week, will all deadlines be met flawlessly? Will sales targets be met? Will quality improve? Will we be on plan? Are you ready to motivate, monitor, and assist each person not only to meet but exceed expectations? Are you ready to hire new recruits and help others move on to greener pastures? Deal with suppliers? Report to your boss or board?

Responsibility for leading a team of people toward a common goal requires an unwavering focus on the end result. As well, there is always reflection back to leadership, structure, and plan: What went wrong last week and why? Will we make up the shortfall this week?

> Your personal vision and leadership skills in delivering the right Plan within the right Structure and with the right People will be tested once again in relation to daily issues that challenge even the most seasoned team manager. There will be things you can control, and others which broadside you. Think of these challenges as opportunities to shine in your calling as a leader.

LEADERSHIP CAN BE A LONELY AFFAIR

As a leader you are often your own Monday morning mentor. It is important to take the time to reflect and reconsider your responsibilities to all stakeholders in relation to this week's activities, and find ways to help your team members become more self-reliant, self-motivated, and balanced in their own approach to their whole life. This requires, an ability to self-assess, and then an action plan that enables you to effectively move the Plan from Point A (last Friday's end results) to Point B (this Friday's achievements) in the short term, while coping with important longer-term issues. To that end, in this part of the book we invite you to consider specific situational examples that will help you:

- Take time to assess and reassess results.
- Address and prevent performance gaps.
- Help top performers excel.
- Connect your team to the big picture.

Chapter 19

GET THE RIGHT FEEDBACK

Real Life

Human beings are hardwired for survival: we would be quivering wrecks, unable to get out of bed in the morning, if we didn't have fairly strong self-esteem and a belief that we are doing lots of things right. But these healthy attributes can also limit our ability to accurately see and evaluate ourselves and our impact on a situation or environment. For example, employee surveys are notorious for reporting that most people believe they are *personally* doing a much better job than everyone else in the company! The reality is that most of us, especially in leadership roles, have a pretty good opinion of ourselves. Failure to see what isn't working, what isn't right, or what is misconstrued because of our emotional attachments, compounds the agony of later defeat. Strong leaders are able to detach themselves from their defined path and reflect accurately on results relating to Plan, Process, and People, by using reliable assessment tools. One of the most important tools is measurable feedback from stakeholders.

THE RIGHT FILTER

One theme in books that deal with communication is that we each have a unique "filter." This filter is created over our life by our experiences and shaped by our personality and current objectives and goals. Everything we see and hear comes through this filter. The result is that you may see and hear something completely different from your colleague across the hall, even though both of you are participants in the same event.

Obviously this filter affects personal decision making, how we receive others' decisions, and how we interpret the feedback we receive, both good and bad. It is not necessary to have a degree in psychology to get the point: we are likely not as self-aware as we think we are, because we really can't absorb every clue that comes our way. People react to us according to their own filters, and we glean out of their reactions whatever our filter lets in. The end result is that we may *think* we are doing a fantastic job, when in reality we may not be impressing those around us. This important limitation on our ability to truly understand our impact on others acts as a major roadblock to making positive change. However, simple acceptance of the fact that our filter may be preventing us from an accurate self-assessment is an important first step to seeking ways to break through this barrier.

TRANSPARENT TEAM FEEDBACK REQUIRED

One of the difficulties leaders can have in assessing results is their reluctance to acknowledge mistakes. By definition, a leader needs to be seen as strong and capable, and the champion of the team's strategy. However, the leader must also be the first person to realize that a change in direction is required. In fact, in both private and public settings, the strongest leaders are often noted for the times in which they admitted to a mistake and their part in it.

This willingness to accept frank assessment, particularly from your team members, can provide critical insights from the front lines, and ultimately allow you to ward off catastrophes that could shake the foundation of the team.

In fact, when processes are proactively put into place to capture personal insights from influential team members and external stakeholders, the resulting culture will be one where it is okay and acceptable to say about even major initiatives, "This ain't working."

On a less dramatic scale, strength is imputed to people who are considered approachable and willing to listen to ideas and suggestions, even those which are contrary to their stated position. Leaders with an aura of approachability implicitly acknowledge the intelligence of the people on the team. Not only will they listen to countervailing suggestions, but they look for ways to tap into the team's advice and guidance, knowing that at the end of it, they alone are in charge and they need to make a decision.

In other words, if you think of the leaders who you really admired and respected, it is likely that you would describe them as confident, yes, but also as people who made you and others on the team feel important and valued precisely because they did not know all the answers. *There is nothing worse for a leader than an environment under which the right information is withheld.*

Carrying this a step further, setting up processes for feedback on your effectiveness is also a demonstration of self-confidence and a sincere desire to participate in achieving Plan success, because if done honestly (i.e., you really intend to accept the good, the bad, and the ugly), looking for ways to continuously improve your personal leadership skills is generally acknowledged as a bold step, and it will motivate those around you to want to do the same.

Just as a strong leader has no need or particular desire to always sit at the end of the table, he or she is also prepared to sincerely hear about the ways or times in which she could be handling a situation differently. In fact, it is feedback that is proactively sought by the leader, within an acceptable and comfortable structure, that is likely to be most successful in positively affecting results.

GETTING THE FACTS

How much feedback you receive as a leader and the form it takes depend on your seniority and the commitment of people around you to assist in your leadership development. As you progress in an organization, feedback is increasingly difficult to obtain. The most extreme example is that of the CEO, a role unlikely to receive anything that remotely sounds or looks like feedback. At that level, the share price of the company is the benchmark, and it is up to the individual to figure out for herself how the company's market value (and the annual compensation granted by the board) translates into what the CEO did well and what he or she needs to do better.

Even at senior levels below the CEO, a leader is expected to be so sufficiently experienced (and compensated!) that he or she neither needs nor expects direct feedback, with the added wrinkle being that the people who report to senior leaders may be intimidated from saying what they really think. The bottom line is that there are challenges at all levels in organizations in receiving useful and timely input on your performance, and it is up to a leader to seek it out.

MENTORING SELF-EVALUATION

A popular approach is for a leader to ask his team members directly for feedback, perhaps in weekly update meetings or after the employee's annual performance review. Questions such as, "What can I be doing better in order to assist you?" are effective, when the leader is an authentic, confident person who practices the A-B-C-D method of leadership style: accountable, bold, caring, and detached.

Whenever you seek useful information from your team members, always remember that regardless of how the question is asked, the respondent usually feels that any answer will sound critical of your performance, and therefore the question will be difficult for people to answer candidly. *However, when properly positioned, questions surrounding improvement of the vision, leadership style, structure, and plan—the usual responsibilities of the leader—provide an opportunity for mentorship.* When leaders receive constructive criticism with grace and use it to improve team efforts, others will be motivated to self-evaluate constructively as well.

Therefore, the best approach is not to view feedback relating to your responsibilities as a separate item focused on *you*, but to see it as your team's overall opinion on how things are going. Viewed from this perspective, such information gathering should involve and include the whole team and be part of an ongoing effort to attain the team objectives. After all, attainment of the team goals and ability as a leader are two sides of the same coin.

Some Personal Insights on Timing and Order of Feedback

After a banner year, it would seem to be a good idea to have a celebration dinner for the staff and their spouses or partners. You and your assistant proceed to organize every detail of an elegant event. After the event, in an effort to obtain feedback you ask the team for their views on it. What you get may not be the team's genuine opinion; after all, the event is over and the bill is paid. Far better feedback would have been obtained if you had initially discussed the planning with the team and solicited their ideas and suggestions. Invariably you will hear something that helps you see a different perspective. The end result is a more engaged team and usually a better outcome.

Historical feedback is not nearly as useful as engaging the team in the original decision-making and planning process. As we discussed in Part 1 of this book, the best way to really engage people in what you and the team need to accomplish is through involvement, which gives rise to the most useful and *forward-looking feedback*.

It isn't necessary or even wise to run every decision by the team: you are the manager and you are being paid for your ideas and your leadership. However, gaining input on significant decisions, preferably through the process created by regular team meetings that people come to rely on, is invaluable. This process eliminates the main problem with getting feedback from your team: that it is too late, in their minds, to be anything but a comment on something that is already over.

FEEDBACK FROM YOUR MANAGER

Just as it is possible to ask your team members for their feedback on the past, you can ask *your* manager for his feedback on how you are doing. If your boss is committed to your development, you may receive some useful coaching and valuable suggestions. However, here again, it is information received after the fact and is therefore of limited usefulness. It is far better to find a way to gain directional input in advance.

Certainly at the outset of working for a new manager, it is well worth your time to ask for regular meetings so that you can most quickly understand what your manager expects from you and how he or she expects these results to be delivered.

Prepare carefully for these meetings, gathering together any materials that will help you quickly explain your ideas and proposed strategies. Then listen carefully for the reaction. You need to come away from these meetings knowing the answer to these questions:

- Are you on the right track with higher-level expectations?
- Are there points that you need to further consider?
- Are there any environmental changes on the horizon from the view at the top?
- Do any of your projects or priorities appear to have lost importance at this time?

The information you can glean from keeping your manager up to date on what you plan to do, and how you plan to do it, will be much more helpful feedback than after you have made a major blunder. As you work with a manager and also as you get more senior in your leadership career, the need to first run things by the boss diminishes. You will get to know exactly what the expectations are and the preferred style. However, savvy leaders at all levels of organizations do tend to keep their boss in the loop, even if informally, to make sure things are still on track. Find out your boss's preferred frequency for such feedback and mentorship opportunities. You'll want his or her undivided attention for a useful exchange, so set up a series of meetings in advance and stick faithfully to that allocation of dates and times.

SUMMING UP

It's pointless—and in fact, damaging to the self-confidence that you need—to measure yourself against managers around you. Although there's a lot to be said for observing and learning from the best practices that are helping others succeed, many people are masters at putting on a good face and talking up their achievements, even to their peers, so what you *think* you see, may not be the real or whole story. You'll simply wind up discouraged and demotivated if you allow yourself to be overly impressed by a surface understanding of any other manager or team.

As well, perhaps you are going through a particularly trying time and you are thinking that it is an impossibly long way from your current state to being and feeling successful. Although you may not fully acknowledge this for a long time, failing, even failing big, is truly the best teacher. However, this only applies if you take the time to really analyze what went wrong, understand and acknowledge what *your* part in the failure was, and consider what you need to do differently.

By being honest about what goes wrong and your part in it, you will be able to see how your behaviors, beliefs, or attitudes negatively affected outcomes so that you can prevent it from hindering the success of future projects. If you are serious about taking time to assess the results of your efforts, put some thought behind how you are going to do that, and from which stakeholders to your Plan you will seek feedback. Then make it easy for people to be honest and candid.

Chapter 20

DON'T JUMP YET: IMPROVE, BUT IN THE RIGHT CONTEXT

Real Life

All too often we read about a media-savvy, charismatic leader espousing on why he is CEO of the Year, only to watch his fortunes or those of his company go down in flames within a year. When it comes to leadership, perfect execution is the impossible dream, and those who claim to be doing it right all the time are likely doomed to failure at some point. Even talking about themselves in that manner suggests they lack the basic humility of the truly great leader.

To be really good at continuous self-improvement, today's leader needs an arsenal of reliable self-assessment tools that begins with an ability to obtain constructive feedback from stakeholders and then interpret it properly.

TAKE A DEEP BREATH

If you believe that there is indeed something to be gained by taking stock of your performance, and you have decided to engage your team in a definitive process to provide feedback, there are many ways to go about this. Preliminary questions for self-reflection and filtering feedback include the following:

- Am I happy in this role?
- Am I getting the results I need?
- Is the Plan being achieved?
- Does the team's structure provide for the greatest amount of involvement by team members?
- Does the communication among other stakeholders, internal and external, enhance productivity?
- Are people in the team self-motivated and really engaged in what they do every day?

Some Personal Insights on Continuous Self-Improvement

High achievers—those who are motivated to improve their position from tenth place to ninth and from second place to first—learn that self-improvement is an ongoing pursuit. They are motivated to reach a plateau and then reach even higher. Consistency in personal development is noticed and sets a leader apart, because it is so difficult. Rather than being motivated by fear, authentic, charismatic leaders are motivated by a need for continuous self-improvement. They also tend to be humble and generous in their approach toward those who help them achieve their goals. It is not uncommon for such leaders to thank *the team* when receiving an award for personal achievements or the team's success.

Although future-looking feedback, direction, and input from both your team and your manager are the two best ways to assess how you are doing, other ideas to consider in obtaining and interpreting feedback are:

- **Self-assessment.** Check out what you already unconsciously know about your direction for self-improvement by writing down three things that you could do over the next six months to make the most positive difference in your work as a leader. Don't think about any of the obstacles that may hinder carrying out these changes; just write them down as if they could be fully implemented tomorrow. Right there you likely have the key opportunities for personal development that would cause your partner, boss, and colleagues (team members and peers) to smile and nod their heads in agreement.

- **Peer feedback.** Asking a trusted peer for feedback can be helpful. Some people are willing to go out on a limb and tell you ways in which you could have obtained a better result or tried a different approach. On the other hand, "trusted peer" often means "friend," so be sure that the person is aware that you really do want the unvarnished truth and *why*. Avoid being "needy" in making the request by confining what you want to know to a narrow and specific event or situation, not requesting an overall, broad-based commentary on how you are doing. Even the most supportive colleague will find that difficult to provide.

- **Client feedback.** Although ostensibly for the purpose of gaining feedback on the organization's level of service, because you are the team leader, this type of client interaction is really about you and your decisions. These surveys, focus groups, and one-on-one conversations often are surprising in their praise and overall satisfaction level, but they will also be sure to tell you exactly what needs to be changed and improved. Reviewed carefully and taken seriously, this candid feedback may indicate some changes you need to make in your leadership style.

- **360-degree survey.** Surveys of the views of your manager, team members, and peers can be highly informative. Implemented and interpreted professionally, these anonymous surveys can help bring some undesired behaviors to your attention. We specifically suggest "professional" support in interpreting 360-degree feedback because this feedback almost always reveals some leadership blind spots that are difficult to understand or accept.

- **Professional coach.** Retaining a professional adviser personally or through the company (if your company offers this benefit) may be extremely helpful. The very best coaches are familiar with your industry and will confront you directly when your perspective on an issue is hindering your progress. The key is to find a person who is well suited to assist you with the development areas that you have at the time. For example, perhaps sales management is an area in which you are struggling. Using a coach whose expertise is in powerful presentations will not get you where you need to be. This is why it is important to first obtain feedback from other sources before looking for and retaining a coach. Many leaders have used the assistance of a professional leadership coach, and once you know the expertise you require, a word-of-mouth referral is often the best route. As you would do in hiring any professional, don't commit to an arrangement until you have met at least a couple of individuals.

- **Observation.** Studying other leaders and managers who are particularly strong in some aspect of their job, can spark awareness of a new approach to try. You need to keep your eyes open for better ways to lead, better ways to communicate, better ways to recognize and reward people, and better ways to address performance gaps. Almost everyone likes to be asked for their views or to share what they do well. For example, let's say you know a peer who is a wizard with numbers and can synthesize the annual business plan in a matter of hours, then make its contents clear to everyone on the team. Observing this may make you realize that your own approach to the planning process is more haphazard and lacks appropriate analysis and understanding. This is an important revelation, making you aware of a limitation that may otherwise not have been obvious to you as a problem. If you decide to go one step further and ask your colleague for some guidance in how he does this review of the plan, you will then be even further ahead.

- **Ongoing training.** Participating continuously in training—whether it is about leadership, personal growth, or technical skills and knowledge—keeps your mind open. New ways to do something or think about an issue can result from new external approaches to training and professional development, without the need to have anyone spell it out for you. Even meeting the instructors and other students may give you fresh insights into how to enhance your leadership ability.

- **Talk to a close friend or partner.** If you are in a situation where you are unsure what to do, sometimes the mere recounting of the issue to a very trusted friend or spouse can clarify the issue in your own mind. The individual may also be able to provide an objective comment or two that pierces through issues clouding your mind. The risk is that the person's judgment is frankly not that good, and the advice you get is even more subjective or lacking perspective than if you were left to your own devices! The only answer to this is time: over time, it will be obvious to you whether that individual's advice served you well, calmed you down, and got you back on track or if the advice lacked the rational insight that you need from a trusted adviser.

SUMMING UP

While there are many complicated ways to measure a leader's effectiveness, the bottom line is that a successful leader's team gets results. Feedback and self-evaluation are important to achieve consistent results over the long term. It can help to devise a personal self-evaluation debrief which you can review following a large project, and before going on to the next one. For example, the following questions flow from the concepts discussed in Responsibility 1: The Leader.

1. Were expectations met? Why/Why not?
2. Did I set high enough standards?
3. Was I honest with the team in following up?
4. Did I treat people with respect?
5. Did I inspire the team?
6. Who was motivated and why?
7. Who was not motivated and why?
8. Were people committed to our success?
9. Did people go the extra mile?
10. Were people able to adapt to change?
11. Were people frustrated or apathetic?
12. Were we able to clue into obstacles?
13. How did we manage and deflect conflict?
14. Was the process flawed in any way?
15. Were results measurable?
16. On a scale of one to ten, to what degree did we get the results we wanted?
17. What would we do differently next time?
18. What would we repeat?
19. How do I feel about starting the next project?

Chapter 21

IF YOU JUST CHANGE
ONE THING...

Real Life

A classic failure in leadership is to allow an otherwise talented member of your team to trip the team up with disruptive behavior. Eventually, with enough disruption, some type of disaster, failure, or forced change will occur, at which point you should have the good sense to consider what went wrong.

If you conclude that it was simply a case of inadequate performance management, you will not have studied the situation carefully enough. The real problem was likely not that you didn't know or understand how to carry out effective performance management, but something more complex such as a desire to be liked or respected by certain people, an issue that is far more likely to test you again in a different way than ineffective performance management.

The need to be liked by most people can limit the effectiveness of your client relationships, hinder your ability to ask for and receive new responsibilities from your boss, and cause you to inadequately advocate for your team. Those are just three examples. Remember that leadership is about the team and about achieving your Plan every time, on time. So take some of the onus off yourself to be perfect and liked by everyone. It's not about you.

WHEN THINGS GO WRONG

So you are at the point of seeing some personal behaviors and attributes that you want to change, either because of the feedback that you have been able to obtain or because it is just plain obvious to the world that things are not going well. Maybe you have been unsuccessful in a role and unceremoniously moved to another job, or perhaps a peer has been suddenly promoted to be your boss for reasons that are, at best, unclear.

Above all, before you think about changing anything, don't whine, don't complain, and don't be indiscreet. You are, after all, a professional change manager, and an expert at managing relationships through good times and bad. Everyone is watching you and the opportunity that the situation gives you is a chance to stand out as a person who gets the collective nod of approval as being a class act.

The bad times will soon be part of the infamously short corporate memory but how you acted, carried yourself, and continued to lead your team will be remembered for a long time. Change yourself, change the situation, or leave… but don't whine, complain, or blame others. It's when things go wrong that the strength of relationships are tested and consolidated. This is a remarkable opportunity for leadership. Use it well.

Beyond that overall advice, there are three things that you can consider taking stock of when looking at the current state of your team and your leadership of it, particularly when circumstances change. These are:

- Being positive and optimistic
- Listening well
- Earning trust

BEING POSITIVE AND OPTIMISTIC

Being optimistic, upbeat, and warm to others even when events and circumstances are challenging are traits of exceptional leaders. Much of Harold Kushner's writing, including his book *When All You've Ever Wanted Isn't Enough*, eloquently points out that life's meaning, for most of us, is not in being the President of the United States or winning the Nobel Prize. Instead, the significance of our lives is most successfully found in the day-to-day pleasures we enjoy and the daily chances we are given to help others or make someone else's life more pleasant. You can think of your leadership in the same light. Especially when times are tough, or something is just not right, it is entirely within your control to convey belief in the people on the team and interest in them as individuals by simple gestures of caring and acknowledgement.

It is in these small things, on the days you find it hardest to get motivated, that your team has the chance to see your leadership in action, not just in the words you say at large meetings or in your title. *In fact, it is when things go wrong that your team needs you and your leadership skills the most.* Working to develop leadership characteristics—consistently enthusiastic and upbeat, self-deprecating and able to easily laugh at yourself, genuinely willing to be open and share your true self—will take you a long way on your desire to be a successful leader. But remember, it is what you do when things go wrong that really counts.

Here is an example:

> Sheila had been running one of the company's stores for five years when management announced that it was time for a change in that location. Sheila was told to look in the head office for a position. Meanwhile, the recruitment process to replace Sheila was put in motion.
>
> Faced with personal uncertainty as to what would happen next, Sheila continued to show up every day and even implemented a new marketing campaign that many people would have left to the next guy. The result? People in the company observing the situation commented on what a "class act" Sheila

was and on the grace that she demonstrated. Not surprisingly, she quickly obtained several offers of employment from various parts of the company. Determined not to let the situation affect her dignity or her character, Sheila's behavior through the experience turned a potentially damaging incident in her career into an opportunity to demonstrate her strength of character.

No matter how prepared you are for the unexpected, understand that some factors affecting your team are beyond your control: your company may have defined pay grades and scales, your financial targets are probably set in the senior executive offices, and the corporate vision may be well beyond your team's mandate. But as a leader, you can't play the victim role. Beyond managing yourself, you manage the team's environment: how the premises look, how people dress, and whether people laugh and joke around before meetings start and treat each other and clients with respect. What has happened above you is only a starting point and, in many cases, is not that influential on whether people are happy and productive in the end. The most influential piece is the immediate team environment, which is controlled by you.

Teams within the same company going through the same difficult takeover can have dramatically different levels of morale. What makes the difference is usually the direct and immediate relationships between the manager and each individual, and the interpersonal dynamics of the team. Is there trust and mutual respect in the group and a feeling of interdependence? What is the culture like? In other words, how do things get done around here and how do we treat each other? These questions are answered at the local level, your area of responsibility, not by the written corporate standards that come from the top of the organization.

LISTENING WELL

The most powerful way to connect with another person is through listening well. But listening well is incredibly difficult, especially when there are difficult issues on your mind. It is a tough task to ignore the flood of thoughts going on in our own head so that we can really hear the thoughts of another.

As managers, we may be busy and impatient, factors adding to the challenge of listening well. This is because the best listeners put the other person at ease, not only through their interested and intense focus on what the person is saying, but also with an unhurried demeanor, a moderate pace of speech and an air of being neither overly emphatic nor opinionated. A listener with these attributes sends out a message of having the time and interest to hear what the speaker really wants to say, improving the chance that the speaker will freely express his thoughts.

Listening is important in assessing your current state of leadership; *becoming a better listener may be the single most important thing you need to do.* In thinking about whether this should be a priority for you, ask yourself:

1. Do you place such an emphasis on good listening that you plan ahead the time and place for important discussions?
2. Do you feel comfortable with negative thoughts and feelings about you being expressed, so that you can continue to listen to them and not interject?
3. Do you make sure that the speaker is completely finished speaking by waiting a few seconds after they stop speaking or asking, "Is there anything more you would like to say about that?"
4. Do you force yourself to simply listen and not to form a reply, solution, or rebuttal while the other person is speaking?
5. Do you make a point of not daydreaming or losing focus on the speaker, even when you don't understand or are not interested in all or part of what he or she is saying?
6. Do you respectfully clarify every point that you do not fully understand?
7. When it is your turn to speak, do you make a point of confirming what you have heard, and if possible and appropriate, do you thank the speaker for their candor/openness/ideas/suggestions?

8. Do you refrain from minimizing the speaker's feelings or reactions by interjecting with comments such as "Don't feel that way...you did a fine job" or "Don't worry, it will work out."
9. Do you avoid launching into an anecdote about a similar situation that happened to you, particularly when the speaker is recounting a difficult or sad situation, for example, the death of a loved one or the diagnosis of serious illness? Rushing in with your own story or health issues, deflates the speaker and blocks further disclosure.

If your responses to any of these questions above give you pause for thought, consider working on your listening skills. Books and courses abound that can help you improve as a listener; like any other skill, the technical concepts about listening well are not as difficult as having the discipline to apply the concepts each and every day.

In our experience, the most important attribute we need as listeners is the sincere intention and desire to give people—such as the people on your team—the gift of your undivided attention. Listening well is a hard thing to fake: you must be genuinely interested in what others think and feel and be driven by a respectful curiosity about their experiences and opinions.

EARNING TRUST

In criminal law, the concept of *intention* means that the same harmful act can have different legal consequences for the perpetrator, depending on whether the act was done intentionally. So, intention has a place in assessing human behavior. However, the best intentions in the world won't help you win the trust of your team if that's all you have. Quite frankly, as a leader of people on a team, intention alone doesn't cut it when it comes to being considered trustworthy.

Some managers pointedly ask the people on their teams to trust them in certain situations and these managers may indeed *intend* to be trustworthy. But remember, it is an ephemeral thing that we call *trust*. People cannot *see* our intentions, our thoughts, or our feelings. People can only see what we *do*, day in and day out.

What is really required to build trust, and manage change? Consider these suggestions:

- **Be clear about your expectations** of people on your team and the team as a whole. Set people up so that they can achieve the expectations, and be there to provide whatever resources or assistance they reasonably need to do that. Follow up consistently when clear expectations are not met. When you follow-up and are disappointed with what you find, don't sugarcoat difficult messages in a blanket of corporate doublespeak. If you are disappointed with an outcome, say so.

- **Be a real person** and open about your reactions and thoughts. While not every reaction to the company's direction may be appropriate to share with your team, don't only parrot the party line. Trust is developed when you are as open as possible about what and how you think.

- **Be unfailingly reliable and true to your word.** If you say you will not repeat something you are told, then don't; after a meeting, send the promised follow-up notes; book dates and organize meetings when you say you will; return messages and don't leave people wondering if you will get back to them or do something; if you set up a meeting or a lunch, don't cancel unless you are ill or a true crisis arises. If you want to be trusted, become known as a person who carries through on commitments, always.

- **Don't be judgmental, rigid, or disrespectful.** Be as open minded to different personalities and diverse opinions as you are open about your own style and your own opinions. Accept that mistakes will be made; over time people will trust that you will stay calm and look for the lesson in a mistake, rather than have an emotional or angry display when the inevitable problems and slipups occur.

SUMMING UP

Your biggest contribution to team success is your ability to continually assess and evaluate and then astutely manage change. With
the right feedback and assessment tools, you and your team can be
successful in an environment of constant change—no matter what
that is—if you can remember your specific roles. The leader's task
is fourfold:

1. To continuously bring the team back to the original vision,
   following defined values and principles.
2. To do so within a defined structure and process that keeps all
   the best interests of every stakeholder in mind.
3. To stick to the Plan, when the original environment prevails,
   but to have the skills to adapt quickly to new environments.
4. To assign the right people at the right time in the right roles.
   This will require a reassessment of original roles and man-
   dates when environments change.

Do It Yourself

Opportunity 1: Taking Time
for Assessment and Evaluation

- **Be open to new ideas and ways to do things.** It is old-
  fashioned and stagnant thinking to rigidly stick to a certain
  leadership style throughout your career. Be open-minded to
  what other managers and leaders are doing that works well
  and consider whether you can implement any of the ideas
  in your own role.
- **Welcome feedback.** Most desirable is feedback that is forward looking. Ask for your manager's and your team's views
  on ideas and plans that you have before these initiatives are
  written in stone. Recognize that if you have recruited

wisely, your team members will have extremely valuable attributes and abilities that you personally do not have; derive the benefits of this talent pool fully.

- **Forgive your failures.** Although the ignominy and disappointment around failing is real and hurtful, if you do it right, failing can transform your leadership career from average to great. Learn everything you can from the event or situation and find a way to prevent a recurrence.

- **Change yourself first.** If things on the team are going badly, look at yourself and your behaviors and actions first. Ask whether a fundamental skill is missing: personal enthusiasm and optimism about the team's mandate, an ability to listen carefully to your team and others, the trust you have earned as a leader. Perhaps before you fix others, you need to fix yourself.

- **Expect others to follow suit.**

OPPORTUNITY 2

PREVENTING AND ADDRESSING PERFORMANCE GAPS

Chapter 22

THE KEY IS IN THE FREQUENCY

Real Life

Preparing performance reviews at year-end is one of the most dreaded managerial responsibilities, right up there with having the year-end meeting. Why is this? One reason is because it has been a full 12 months since the last sit-down meeting and last written assessment. No doubt the manager is painfully aware that there are issues that would have been better discussed months ago, not left until year-end.

When meetings and conversations are frequent and regular, just the frequency and regularity of the same old questions is usually enough to get even the biggest procrastinator or otherwise ineffective performer to take action. To avoid having to say again that the report has not been written, the team member with a tendency to delay will quickly learn that the report needs to be on time. Every team member will simply become accustomed to doing whatever he or she needs to do. A stern voice, harsh words, and uncomfortable conversations

> are unnecessary and even out of place when you have set in motion a cycle of constant two-way feedback about what's been achieved and what has not.

Performance issues, top-notch or disappointing, can and should be addressed on an ongoing basis within the context of your regular process and structure, as we discussed in Responsibility 2. In fact, the issues on both sides of the equation, positive and negative, tend to become exposed, quite without fanfare, in the context of team accountability. In a dynamic team, "tolerations" either never start or are addressed immediately through peer review and performance expectations.

REGULAR MEETINGS, REPORTING MANDATORY

The V-Team structure described in Responsibility 2 provides an ideal structure for weekly or monthly operational meetings. It can be used to require each team member to take a place at the planning and implementation table, ensure their ongoing active participation in projects, and a formal time-regulated forum to bring out their best innovative ideas and experience in support of the Plan. In addition, this is an ideal place to interpret the numerous communications from all stakeholders and the field of play—your interaction with your immediate client base—and to report on accountabilities and results. When the spotlight is centered each week on each engaged team member, reporting on deadlines and results becomes a routine energizer for the team. A positive side effect are the opportunities for informal leadership and self-assessment given to each member of the team.

THE BEAUTY OF ONE-ON-ONES

When you structure your weekly or monthly collaboration process to include a regular one-on-one discussion with each team member, momentum for Plan achievement can really build and unexpected obstacles are controlled. If a problem arises or a team member begins to perform in an unsatisfactory way, you will already have an existing process in place to address it quickly and effectively.

For this to work effectively, however, scheduling regular meetings right from the first day that you become the manager is essential. Getting the dates for these regular updates into your calendar for the next six months immediately eliminates the angst accompanying setting up a "talk" when something is going sideways. Booking a meeting out of the blue is much more likely to start the discussion off on the wrong (defensive, tense) note than a discussion during your regular "Wednesday at 2" meeting time.

Regularly scheduled meetings do not mean that you don't talk frequently with people throughout the week, or that the meetings may get cancelled occasionally because the group meeting covered all the things going on with that person. It simply means that you have a *process* in place. For the most part, this process will provide you with a built-in forum for asking questions and gaining clarity whenever a gap develops between the results you need and the results being delivered.

ON SLICK PERFORMANCE PLANS

The other essential requirement to controlling unanticipated results within the team or from individual performance is the benefit of establishing crystal-clear annual performance plans. Often corporate performance-related documentation is too wordy, describing every possible activity that the individual may ever do. Thanks to cut-and-paste options in word processing, these documents often build up, year over year, until no one even bothers reading them! It's fine to start with a previous document as a base, but be sure to pare it down to essentials.

Ask yourself:

- What do I really expect this person to deliver this year?
- What does the team really need him or her to do?

- On what criteria will I assess his or her rating and the bonus he or she receives?
- Exactly how will this person's performance integrate with and impact the team?

The key performance indicators for the year need to be spelled out in a clear, specific, and measurable way, defining both qualitative factors (how will it get done? How will relationships be managed?) and quantitative benchmarks (hard numbers). A great way to get some momentum around these annual performance plans is to meet with individuals first to get their thoughts and buy in, and then to kick off the year with a team retreat or event to discuss how individuals, the team as an individual entity, and the team leader will work together to get the results everyone wants. The idea of weekly meetings, updates, and performance management may not sound exciting or glamorous, but a strong, consistent communication process is at the core of leadership and essential to your satisfaction as a manager.

Chapter 23

I'LL JUST IGNORE IT ...
THIS ONE TIME

Real Life

Our work as leaders reflects our entire past experience. Nowhere is this more apparent than when a leader has an underperforming team member. Some leaders were raised to believe that it is important to be "nice" and not to offend others. These leaders tend to avoid dealing with underperformance at all costs. They worry about offending the other person, or they conclude that it simply isn't worth the hassle to have what they see as a confrontational conversation.

In contrast, other leaders who grew up playing competitive team sports will have learned the importance of standing up for themselves and that rough physical contact (within the rules) has nothing to do with being friends after the game is over. It is interesting that often a manager with a background in competitive athletics can draw an analogy between the playing field and the workplace, and thus be better equipped to address performance issues. However, any skill can be learned, and having challenging conversations that address underperformance is no exception.

ADDRESSING TOLERATIONS

In an ideal team in the ideal environment, performance issues never arise. After you have painted a clear picture of your expectations to each team member, the team creates and implements a successful action plan to achieve those goals. Similarly in the perfect world, your own focus on the Plan is unwavering, your self-discipline exemplary. But there is no ideal workplace, anywhere, anytime. As much as we like to espouse principles such as "Every person is worthwhile," some people simply are not committed to the goals and values of the team. Furthermore, although there is great benefit to being a supportive coach as a manager, the reality is that even the best coach cannot turn around every troublesome situation.

The point is that there is no perfect state in management, and at some point in your career, sooner or later, you and your team will be held back from your optimal success because of what you, as the leader, are willing to tolerate. In other words, although you may get mad about these tolerations, privately fuming over them, you allow them to continue. Why is this? To an extent, we have become a society of conflict avoiders. These days we are hesitant to fail an elementary or high school student in fear of damaging the child's self-esteem. And when performance gaps arise in the workplace, too often we let things slide until the only option is an expensive severance package.

At times it appears that in the workplace, we are afraid of offending people with comments that may be taken the wrong way, even if those comments are critical to the short- and long-term success of both the individual and the team. The result is that intelligent, capable, and otherwise successful managers can become confused and worn down by an issue that they are tolerating. They expose themselves to an erosion of focus that can be so severe that they lose their way, becoming too exhausted or frustrated to return to Plan.

Leaders who avoid troublesome situations for an extended time are embarking on a "hope trip"—they hope that they can get the results they want and need without confrontation. This rarely happens. Instead they end up seriously off track or in the gutter.

SORRY, AVOIDANCE JUST WON'T CUT IT

Clint Eastwood was right when he said, "Sometimes if you want to see a change for the better, you have to take things into your own hands." Team leaders must take control and this includes addressing underperformance by individuals on the team. While this can be difficult and even unpleasant for many managers, good leaders know that avoiding these matters wastes resources and the entire team risks failure. Most people don't like confrontation and try to avoid it. Here are some common reasons:

- **The Likeability Factor.** You are overly concerned about being liked by everyone, and in fact, you may even have been trying to gain consensus on all decisions so that everyone likes not only you but also your decisions! But applying a "perfection" standard is not a valid self-assessment tool, and cheats your team of clear thinking.

- **The Noise Factor.** You are worried about the person's reactions when you raise problems with performance: Will the individual become emotional, cry, scream, or throw things? Will he quit? Will word of your difficult conversation get into the grapevine and jeopardize your relationship with other team members, other colleagues in the company, or even in the community?! The real issue is one of control. Who is in control? Who needs to be in control? Who is the master of the Plan and accountable for its results? In these situations a healthy ego is paramount. Do not succumb to manipulative behaviors that put you and the team off Plan now and in the future.

- **The Deep Breath Factor.** You are concerned about managing your own feelings. You are unsure how you will react to an angry or devastated person. Maybe you have had a bad experience in the past when a performance discussion became a heated exchange during which you made statements you later regretted. Take a deep breath, concentrate hard and accept that sometimes leadership is all about managing one's own behavior in difficult situations.

WHEN TOO MUCH BAGGAGE PUTS YOU AT RISK

There are many ways we cover up our fears to justify our persistent reluctance to confront, wasting precious time, resources, and energy.

Do these excuses sound familiar?

- "She has lots of good qualities; I can deal with her negative characteristics."
- "I should not have to tell people how to do their jobs."
- "He has a lot of difficult things going on in his life right now."
- "I'm sure this will pass ... he has always been a strong performer in the past."
- "If I say anything, he will tell everyone; it just isn't worth losing sleep over it."
- "It's a tough job to fill ... maybe I couldn't find anyone else who is even as good."
- "It's too much work to go through HR's process around here!"

Behind all of these excuses lie thoughts and beliefs from our upbringing and our past experience—what is and isn't appropriate to do and say to others. But as leaders we must leave that baggage behind. To lead a workplace that is respectful of everyone and their contribution, the leader must recognize not only those who contribute a lot but also those who frankly do not pull their weight. To leave a problem unchecked creates tension and anxiety, not to mention the immediate poorer results. Let's be clear. Failing to take action will inevitably torpedo your team, your career, or both.

For the person or people who manage *you*, it will become not only a performance issue about your underperforming employee, but more importantly, a leadership issue about you. You will be seen as indecisive and weak, and the people who have been strong performers on the team may potentially lose respect for you and the organization. Retention of key employees is placed at risk.

Wherever you are on the spectrum from complete avoidance to aggressive and immediate confrontation, the message is the same: dealing with underperformers appropriately and effectively can make or break your career.

In short, the reason it is so essential to address underperformance by your team members sooner, rather than later, in today's competitive global marketplace is that no individual acting alone can achieve a team's whole plan. It simply can't be done; productivity targets simply cannot be met. The leader's greatest opportunity for success lies in rallying each individual team member's efforts into a unified result. That result will be—you guessed it—greater than the sum of its parts. As much as that sounds like a worn out homily, our experience, both personally and from observing other leaders, is that holding people accountable is done far less often than it needs to be.

SUMMING UP

How do you hold people accountable for their performance and help them make the right decisions as it relates to their performance and achieving the overall Plan? How do you ensure that one team member does not sabotage themselves, their team members, or your career through manipulative behaviors?

Being an agreeable and well-liked leader obviously contributes much to one's success; however, leading a team that works harmoniously is paramount to leadership success in business today. When a team is jeopardized by negative behaviors or underperformance by some team members, we cannot get the results we want and need.

In thinking about team harmony, consider these action plans:

- Be prepared for potential scenarios of concern by first reviewing your company's human resource policies. Know your company's rights, your rights, and those of your team members. Always take this into account in preparing your team structure and plan.

- Beyond this, ensure that expectations of the team and the individuals on the team are clearly articulated and periodically repeated.
- Make sure that everyone understands and gels within the team culture and the fact that only together will they be able to reach productivity goals.
- Provide a structure for regular individual and team meeting time that anticipates and works toward results on a proactive rather than a reactive basis.
- Be ready and willing to address underperforming team members long before their poor performance threatens the team's success.

Chapter 24

GETTING OFF THE HOPE TRIP EXPRESS

Real Life

The pivotal moment of deciding to act on an intolerable situation is often when you realize that most of your crises feature the same person or same occurrence. When most of the frustrating moments in your day relate back to one individual or one process going wrong, you know you have a problem.

When this type of realization concerns a team member, chances are good that in between the crisis situations, you observe some good, maybe even excellent, performance. But eventually all these good moments are just helping you duck the reality that this is not a "high maintenance" team member; this is an instance of the warranty being expired. It's time to act.

The good news is that recognizing your "tolerations" is at least half the battle. Once you see them clearly as unreasonable impediments to your team goals, the right answer as to what to do can usually be found fairly quickly. The bad news is that there are usually compelling reasons why you have not fully accepted these tolerations as thorns in the team's side, and so there is a good chance that you will allow them to persist.

For example, in today's high-performance corporate environment, high-achieving, smart, extremely competent, technically savvy *individuals* are often hired and thrown together as a team. The expectation is that the team of high-performers will be a high-performing team (makes sense, doesn't it?!) but too often, these teams fail. The team is described as "not jelling," or being overly "political" or "dysfunctional." Many times when these buzz words are used, the real issue is that the manager is ducking one or more tolerations.

You may know immediately the tolerations that you have in your work right now. Great! Take action and carry on. On the other hand, you may be so worn down by your personal "hope trips" that you don't recognize them for what they are: matters requiring your immediate attention. One question to ask yourself is whether your job is one you love, or whether it is highly stressful. Even high pressure, challenging management work should be enjoyable. If instead you are experiencing ongoing stress that you cannot turn off when you walk out of the office at night, then you have a problem and it is likely something or someone that you are putting up with when you should instead draw the line in the sand.

If you are still unsure whether you have any unacceptable tolerations going on in your own job right now, try these exercises:

1. List the five things that could happen in the next month that would best propel your team to greater success. If you say, "The best thing that could happen to the team is if Kristie left," then clearly you are just tolerating Kristie's performance or attitude. Or if you say, "The best thing that could happen is if we had $50 million in offshore sales," then the toleration likely is the activities and behaviors of the offshore sales team.
2. List the things that, if changed, would most reduce your stress in your job.

3. Are there people or topics that you dwell on when you talk (complain!) about your work to your partner or best friend? Is this trusted person often urging you to "just fix it"?
4. Is there anyone on your team that when he or she comes through your door, your anxiety level goes up?
5. List those meetings in your typical week that cause you uneasiness rather than a feeling of moving your team's agenda ahead.
6. List the tasks that you personally are doing that really should be done by someone else.
7. List the activities that you are not finding the time to do that are important to your job (think: sales activity management, meeting prospects and clients, coaching the best performers on your team ...). Then ask yourself: *What am I doing instead that is preventing me from doing these important activities?*

DON'T STEW IN YOUR JUICES

Once you realize that you need to take action, take time to reflect on the situation and plan your strategy. Reflection before action is important. You were given a management position because of demonstrated success in your career, so clearly you are competent and smart, and allowing unreasonable situations fester is not considered a smart thing to do.

For that reason, you owe it to yourself to ask why have I, with my proven track record, let this situation develop and continue? Call upon the available resources in your company to assist you. Make sure your manager and the human resources group are part of your planning process. At times working in a structured corporate environment can be challenging with its many departments, but when you need to address a toleration situation, the support that your organization offers may be invaluable. These services can also be subcontracted by those firms not large enough to support a human resources department. Now is the time to rally that support.

HAVE A PLAN TO DEAL WITH TOLERATIONS

A step-by-step plan for dealing with your tolerations may look something like this, using your A-B-C-D Model of Leadership Style:

- **Be accountable.** Plan the meeting carefully with the help of your support resources such as someone in your human resources group.
- **Be bold.** Know what you will say and how you will say it, what you won't say no matter how emotional the meeting gets, and what you need to achieve by the meeting's end. Plan to use your team members' emotional retorts and denials, or withdrawal and sullenness, as valuable opportunities to move the discussion ahead. By becoming angry, defensive or silent, your team member is actually giving you a chance to ask questions about his reactions and find out more about the problem. Perhaps there is a relevant fact that you need to know. Now is not the time for you to retaliate with emotional statements of your own. It is hard to regain the meeting's direction and balance if you, the leader, let the discussion become mired in rhetoric and heated words.
- **Be caring.** You are a decent person; let that shine through as you discuss what is right for every stakeholder impacted by the team. Work to a specific outcome in the meeting. You will have decided on this outcome in advance. If a significant piece of information has come out of the discussion, you may need to adjust the expected results, but one way or another the meeting must end with an agreement for some change or improvement. *Be clear.* Do you need to see an immediate change in behavior or performance or simply a plan for how the improvements will be made? What are the consequences of making or not making the changes?
- **Be detached.** In the meeting, be as detached as possible, meaning that you will sit back and as much as possible, be an observer and a careful listener. Use very recent and concrete examples of the tolerated behavior and indicate that it will

not be tolerated any longer. In a meeting where emotions run high, the upper hand goes to the individual who does not "react" but instead "acts." In taking the seconds or minutes to absorb what is happening, you can think of the appropriate response that will allow you to stay on your meeting plan. You will recognize that extraneous or irrelevant statements for what they are, and calmly reiterate the topic under discussion.

Follow up the initial confrontational meeting with consistent actions and words. Your understanding of the meeting should be put in writing, including the agreed outcomes with dates as to when various steps will be taken or changes made. Then "inspect what you expect." Make sure commitments are met, including any commitments you made, such as providing additional training or support.

Continue to involve the people and parties whom you consulted before the meeting. Monitor the success of dealing with the toleration in conjunction with them and let them know you appreciate their support and assistance. Recognize positive changes made and work toward establishing a strong relationship with the individual. But stay on top of the situation to prevent any backsliding into another similar situation.

Do It Yourself!

Opportunity 2: Preventing and Addressing Performance Gaps

- **Stay aware of tense, difficult situations that you are tolerating for some reason.** Find out why things are happening in the group and address unacceptable results before they bring down the team.
- **Try to be boring.** In other words, establish a process for communicating regularly with each team member so

that it is never a big deal to have a meeting. Instead, you can talk about what each member of the team is doing before anything becomes a problem, and if there are gaps in performance, you can gently direct the individual back on track.

- **Have confidence in yourself and your track record.** If your diligent efforts at adhering to a process and structure are not achieving the desired results, then step back and reconsider who is not doing what. In every employee–employer relationship, each party must give, on average, 50 percent of the required elements. Maybe it is time to stop thinking that you need to do more and start thinking that your team member needs to be held accountable.

- **Use available resources to address underperformers and intolerable situations.** Prizes aren't awarded for the manager who never needs help. Trained consultants or staff people in your organization may be able to assist you in recognizing problems for what they are, setting an action plan to deal with them, and preparing for a difficult discussion.

- **Follow up faithfully.** Remember, always follow up when extraordinary performance management steps have been taken. All your time and effort is wasted if you drop the ball and never follow up on which of the agreed changes have been made.

OPPORTUNITY 3

MANAGING TOP PERFORMERS EFFECTIVELY

Chapter 25

WE'VE COME A LONG WAY, BABY

Real Life

In the 1950s and 1960s, Peter Drucker coined the term, *knowledge worker*, referring to those providing intellectual ability rather than physical labor. Drucker pointed out that each knowledge-based employee makes a distinctly individual contribution, much more varied than is usually found in physical labor, which by its nature is generally simpler in terms of required skill sets and work environments.

Today, knowledge workers often work in virtual workplaces, such as in a taxi with a wireless e-mail device, and the community of people involved in this work is often global. Managing people in this environment is a more complex task than when Drucker first identified knowledge as a commodity; today it's about the individual *and* the team, serving a global marketplace, often electronically. Top performers must not only be technically skilled but they must also possess a high degree of emotional intelligence and communication skills.

THE OPPORTUNITY FOR THE KNOWLEDGE MANAGER

As technology makes the world a faster—and smaller—place, we value more greatly the "soft skills." To have the potential to advance, top performers must be well read, articulate in writing speaking, organized, sincere, energetic... This list goes on! In short, there must be a fire burning, a passion for the work, a vision or a purpose that drives the candidate to higher heights along with exemplary people skills. Your job as a manager is to recruit for these traits and to develop them in each individual on your team. There is no place for arrogant individuals with an ego-driven me-first focus in today's work environment; what you want to avoid is the employee who takes all the credit, blames others, or fails to take responsibility. These behaviors can be fatal to your objective of building a successful team.

The importance of smart recruitment is magnified by the size of the community served by your team. The broader your team's universe, the more essential it is to have stellar ambassadors. View this as an opportunity for astute recruitment and the development of the required attributes of personal integrity and team collaboration skills. In carrying out your responsibility for the people on your team, you must merge the needs of the individual with the expectations placed on your team. *This requires both reciprocity—the mutual exchange of benefits within a relationship that are to the advantage of both the employer and the business—and a clear understanding of what is negotiable and what is not when it comes to delivering bottom-line results.* Nowhere will your abilities as a skillful relationship manager be tested more than in your dealings with top performers. In order to motivate, train, and retain highly skilled people, you must recruit and cultivate top talent both from within your organization and from external sources.

MANAGING RISING AND DIMMING STARS

Top performers or exceptional achievers are considered to be rare and valuable assets. They can also be difficult to lead. One of the reasons for this is that top performers are leaders themselves, and this differentiates them from the rest of the team. By their nature they are often *not* team players—and teamwork can be both puzzling and painful for them. However, you can successfully integrate top performers into a team structure by getting them engaged in leadership activities. They are tremendously effective and powerful members of advisory councils, for example, and innovative thinkers relating to how to measure performance and potential market growth opportunities. However, while it is certainly true that your top performers can do much to assist your team in achieving its Plan, the aura around top performers can also have detrimental consequences.

The grading or ranking systems so often used within organizations can make your assessment of a top performer challenging, particularly that of a person whom you have inherited rather than recruited. For example, top performers can be incredibly strong in one or more areas, but weak in others. So although assessment tools of any type can provide valuable insight, you need to be wary of accepting labels as gospel, forgiving top performer shortcomings, allowing top performers to monopolize your time, and failing to recognize other high performers.

1. **Accepting the "gospel" about top performers.** There are many reasons why people get labeled as stars in the company and not all of them are necessarily valid. For example, some team members are exceptionally good at currying favor with their managers and saying whatever it is that the manager wants to hear. In some managers' view, this is the essence of a "star." In other cases you may find that a person on your team simply has the gift of a golden tongue, or the "schmooze" factor, such as speaking eloquently in meetings, particularly when senior management is around.

   We are not suggesting that currying favors with the boss and schmoozing well with senior management always indicate that the individual is not a top performer. Unfortunately, some very talented people have the annoying tendency to be obsequious.

If that's the case, over time all you need to do is encourage the go-getter to tone down the behaviors that do not contribute to the team dynamics and are almost certainly not helpful to him or her in the long run. But there is also the possibility that underneath the bluff, bluster, and right things to say, that much-praised team member you have taken on to manage is not a star. Likely your assessment has uncovered issues that have been ignored for a long time and sorely require addressing.

2. **Overlooking or forgiving the shortcomings of top performers.** We have suggested that not everyone who is introduced to you as a star may in fact really be a star. You need to keep your eyes and mind open. But of course there is little doubt that among those who have been identified as top performers, some truly are exceptionally good at what they do. Year in and year out they contribute in a very important way to the team's success, often in the sales they produce or the difficult projects they implement.

   The trap here, however, is in ignoring their shortcomings. Prior managers may have turned a blind eye to significant performance issues, often in the area of interpersonal skills, including appropriate behavior. The reason? Because the star's ability to make the sale, woo the client, or otherwise "put the puck in the net" is coveted by the organization. The gaps in performance or behavior apart from this talent are accepted as part of the star's price. In the big picture of developing your team to its maximum potential, overlooking these gaps is usually a mistake. Often, turning a blind eye to a star's idiosyncrasies and unproductive habits is a surefire way to create disharmony in the team, limit overall results, and lower team morale.

3. **Accepting the commonly held view that top performers should take up the majority of your time as a manager.** The so-called 80–20 rule is often touted as the way to spend your time as a manager: 80 percent of your time should be spent on the 20 percent of your team who contribute exceptional results. There is a lot to be said for setting goals together with

the stars and touching base with them frequently, but beyond that, they often prefer to have as much autonomy as possible. Believing that you trust them to continue to excel is very important to most high achievers. As well, by focusing primarily on your top people, you may overlook the underperformers and the average-to-above-average team members. Underperformers need sufficient attention to either (a) turn their performance around, or (b) help them leave what is obviously the wrong job.

4. **Don't Ignore the Twinkling Stars.** Worse than blithely accepting the corporate notion that someone is a star, is the error of overlooking some terrific people as the stars that they truly are. People overlooked as top or exceptional performers are typically hard-working, smart, loyal, positive thinkers, even in the face of change or transition. These unsung heroes perhaps carried on, for example, in the months before you were appointed as the team's manager; this type of person carries on doing a great job even with no one at the helm.

   You may be thinking, why would people like that be overlooked? The answer is the opposite of why some so-called stars really aren't stars: just as those types often rely on their ability to be articulate and self-promoting, the unnoticed top performers shy completely away from calling attention to themselves. Their stellar and creative work, their skills, and their potential go unnoticed, sometimes for years. Their pleasant and perhaps low-key approach works *against* them in the sense that few people recognize their talents. Watch carefully for these people; *they are your secret assets*.

   This category of individuals provides you with a tremendous opportunity to showcase your ability to develop talent. It is often the workhorses today who are the top team players of tomorrow. These "key resources" are consistent, solid performers who merit your attention as you plan your structure and processes.

   These people can also assist you in carrying out an analysis of the good, the bad, and the ugly in the team's processes and results. Ask for their opinions and input. Find out what is missing in their job satisfaction levels; perhaps it is not much. In fact, the biggest problem in this group might be complacency. It is possible that previous managers did not provide an environment for goal achievement or performance enhancement. Your new thoughts on increasing productivity may therefore seem intimidating at first. Always make a point of considering performance markers and rewards that are meaningful, given that the individual performers are not necessarily driven by the need to be top performers, but may instead be highly motivated by being part of a successful group. *Today's team players are tomorrow's top performers.* They are your key to increased productivity.

To build meaningful relationships with the solid performers doing the lion's share of the team's work, consider introducing the concept of a participative management system around a V-Team or similar structure as discussed in Responsibility 2. You may wish to do this on an individual basis first, or in a team retreat environment, followed up by individual one-on-one meetings. When the unsung heroes understand that this structure provides them with a forum for input, they will likely be both motivated and excited. Most people like to be listened to and to do important, meaningful work.

When everyone is accountable, and provided with the chance to voice a personal vision, group leadership just happens...and so does its recognition and celebration. Particularly in managing relationships with potential top performers, recognize that they warrant ongoing, personalized, and specific feedback about the work that they do and the contribution they make to the team. Often this group is highly regarded by customers and can provide the team with "touch points" to important competitive intelligence. High sales performers usually possess considerable day-to-day street smarts. Be sure to find a process and a structure within which to capture this knowledge and a rewarding platform for building and retaining your relationship with them.

SUMMING UP

Nurturing top performers can be a daunting, ongoing task. By setting developmental standards, performance targets, educational opportunities, and innovative reward structures, you will enable top performers to flourish. Over time, the best people will seek out your team as the one to work for. Moreover, making sure that a plan for personal growth is available to top performers can be critical in the successful management of these relationships. Top performers like to work for leaders who are:

1. Respectful of that top performer's time.
2. Available, reliable, responsive, and trustworthy, because the top performer typically sets high standards for the boss.
3. Worthy of mentorship: that is, the leader will want to be able to demonstrate success in his or her own right.
4. Insightful, and confident enough to be both bold and detached in making recommendations for the top performer's improvement. Top performers will especially respect this if your mentorship is of value to them. Don't tell them what they already know; share what you have learned from your experiences that may be relevant to their success.

Consider the following within the context of your personal leadership style and approaches:

1. How do I evaluate top performers?
2. How do I develop objective performance criteria which are challenging and respectful of the top performer's own standards?
3. How do I provide the right environment for top producers to develop and progress within the structure of the team and the context of the Plan?
4. How do I best tap into the low-lying fruit: those quiet potential top performers who work consistently without recognition?

Besides your own leadership style, your other three responsibilities around the management of top performers must also be carefully evaluated:

1. **Structure.** The right team structure is important. You need to balance the "open architecture" desired by top performers having an independent streak with the needs of the rest of the team.
2. **Performance to plan.** By their continuous need for self-improvement, nurturing the talent of top performers requires special insight. Strive to provide an environment for intellectual and personal growth and personal influence. Get these people engaged in leadership.
3. **People and team.** Find a way to integrate top performers into the team culture. Your team needs to be a place where people with a range of skills and aspirations can feel energized.

Chapter 26

THE DELUSIONS OF TOP PERFORMERS

Real Life

The threat posed by top performers is their ability to take over a team, make a team all about them and their successes, even sway the manager to thinking that what the top performer wants, he gets.

One highly successful professional hockey coach is known for his insistence on the team doing it his way: when training camp starts, everyone gets a haircut and certain training regimes and schedule restrictions are nonnegotiable. Why does he do this? One reason is likely the tendency for sports team to have a "star" or two . . . a gifted athlete, no doubt, but potentially disruptive to the team by his or her attitude and expectations.

By virtue of their incredible talent, top performers can have personal idiosyncrasies that present incredible management challenges. The opportunity for leaders lies in the ability to coach people away from limiting behaviors.

In our experience, top performers can harbor one or more of three delusional beliefs about their individual status:

1. Personal habits don't matter.
2. Career progression will be twice as fast as what the company has in mind.
3. Work-life balance is achievable at the same pace as career ambitions. These beliefs must be carefully considered in relation to the team environment you want to cultivate.

PERSONAL HABITS MATTER

Aware that they are recognized for their potential to take on larger positions, the stars that you manage may believe that personal habits don't matter. Rules about personal habits, such as what we wear and how we act, have become sensitive topics.

It is hard to know exactly when and how it happened, but many of the etiquette and dress guidelines that once applied to society generally, in both work and at home, now seem outdated. But what has become accepted by society at large may not be as acceptable in the workplace. Or a better way to state that may be to note that the top performers you manage need to know that to achieve their most ambitious career goals, they would be well advised to learn some old-fashioned manners and deportment.

Some Personal Insights on Erosion of Decorum

Business etiquette—language, dress and professional formality—is important. It really pays to keep communications with all stakeholders, at the highest possible level of business etiquette. You just can't err being overly respectful. This can be particularly challenging when there is an emotionally charged issue, when you feel you are being treated unfairly, or when there is an issue of control. Stop and think. Take that time; it's important. Know your manners. Never drop down to the lowest common denominator. Never, ever swear. Be known for that. It takes a very long time to recover from the erosion caused by anger or coarse language. Keep your eye on the ball; know your final negotiating position, but have the discipline to employ respectful language and behavior, no matter how you are provoked.

CAREER PROGRESSION EXPECTATIONS

The speed at which some high achievers expect to advance is a perennial concern to managers. The definition of patience by many high achievers is waiting for a promotion until next week rather than this week! It is important for both the organization and the exceptional individual that you help them understand what is reasonable and possible, in an encouraging and positive way. The temptation may be to paint a slightly rosier picture than the probable career path. Don't do this. If anything, be more conservative in your forecasts and be sure to emphasize the work that is needed to be done to get there. Lay out clearly the exceptional results that the person needs to achieve and keep achieving.

The fundamental purpose of a team is to achieve its Plan. The same is true for an individual to succeed: to move on to more responsibility and greater challenge, he must first excel at the current position. It is easy for high performers to lose focus on their work by some early success. Unfortunately, this can delay future progression until they either realize on their own *the importance of succeeding along the way* or a caring and committed manager begins to work with them.

ACHIEVING WORK-LIFE BALANCE ALONG WITH CAREER AMBITIONS

Unless you have come up against this issue in your managerial role, you may find it hard to believe that the top performers we have been describing—ambitious, impatient, driving personalities—may also expect balance in their overall lives. *Balance* is a relatively new phenomenon that is a viable concept for the many people who truly want to have equal attention and equal success in their personal and work lives.

A good example is a parent who chooses to spend significant time with his or her child or children, maybe on a part-time basis or simply by leaving work at a regular time each night. Although perhaps not as perfect as being there for the child 100 percent of the time, they see it as a viable compromise.

However, it is difficult for some people to recognize that lifestyle choices carry consequences on the work front. Just as the children won't have a full-time dad or mom, the workplace is not getting someone contributing at the level of a fast tracker, so it is unreasonable to expect the fast tracker's pace, pay, or perks.

In the interest of attracting and retaining great people, some organizations are prepared to overlook unequal contributions. These organizations will reward and recognize all people on the team in the same way, regardless of the personal-work balance they choose. There are both benefits and costs to employers who make the choice to treat all employees equally regardless of contribution. Although it may sound appealing in the recruitment process, in practice, the harder-working team members are likely to become disgruntled and leave for an organization where compensation and advancement are determined on merit.

The wise manager—the one who really cares about an ambitious top performer—will help him understand that every choice has consequences. The choice to have a life that is consistently balanced does not line up with rapid advancement, regardless of what is stated in the employee manual's policies and procedures. Real life diatates that some jobs simply demand a lot of time and effort.

In conclusion, in managing top performers, at some point you will be required to candidly address their "delusions." One person who outperforms an entire team is valuable indeed. However, the nonnegotiables are still there: appropriate personal habits, an understanding of the organization's ability to move them ahead, a willingness to contribute equally to the team's success. *Everyone within a team deserves respectful behavior from the others.* As the leader, you need to manage team dynamics carefully as it relates to top performers, within your operating structure and vision.

SUMMING UP

"There's no feeling quite like the one you get when you get to the truth: You're the captain of the ship that called you. You're setting the course, the speed, and you're out there on the bridge, steering." This quote by Carl Frederick underscores the essence of spirit within the top performer, who can be a vital team member, or drop out—depending on how well you lead. One thing is for certain: prima donna behavior simply no longer works in today's environment. *One person alone cannot possibly achieve today's productivity expectations of a whole teams.* Therefore the delusions of top performers must be recognized and corrected when they threaten the team's overall success.

A "team of one" must develop over time into a high-performing member of a well-tuned respectful "team of many." Your role as leader is to show the top performer how to work well with the rest of the team, while retaining his or her edge. Your personal confidence in providing firm but friendly guidance will help your top performers become better liked and respected by team members who may otherwise find them overbearing and overdemanding.

Chapter 27

A CHECKLIST FOR
MANAGING YOUR STARS

Real Life

The primary theme of this book is that productivity targets cannot be met by one individual, but rather they can only be achieved by a fully engaged team. You want your team to look forward to coming to work in the morning, to believe at the end of a week that they did or created something meaningful and to know at year-end that they have made a difference. This is particularly important for your "stars."

Almost by definition, a top performer cares deeply about what she contributes. It is likely that she derives a significant amount of her overall life satisfaction from her work and looks to you, perhaps unconsciously, to play a considerable role in keeping her job fresh and interesting.

Ensuring that people on the team, especially the best performers, are constantly engaged in what they are doing is not difficult but it does require attention and thought, such that you must keep the goal of involving and consulting people uppermost in your mind.

In either category, there are often individuals who have not yet demonstrated to you and the organization that their self-assessments are accurate. For example, a person with an expectation of taking on your job one day may or may not have shown that ability; in fact, he may have demonstrated clearly that he is not capable of the role. Similarly, an individual doing a fantastic job of being a relationship manager in a pharmaceuticals company may be seen by the company as having the potential to manage a team, and yet she has expressed no interest or inclination to take on a management position.

In addition to the cardinal rule of having a clear understanding of expectations between the organization and the high performer, six additional guidelines will enhance the management of your team's top performers:

1. **Soar higher, together.** There are always projects, tasks, meetings, informational emails, and reports that managers get assigned, given, sent . . . whatever the mode of delivery and communication, the stream is relentless! So share it! What seems mundane and uninteresting to you may be inspiring and of great interest to a high performer on your team. *You* don't need to personally attend every meeting, be on every corporate task force, and show up at every client reception.

2. **Spread the wealth.** If ego holds you back from being more open with information, events, and projects then ask yourself why and get over it. Surrounding yourself with terrific people who are all working on projects that interest them creates the best results for the team. As the leader, you are assessed on the results of the *team*, not what you, personally,

can get done in a day. It is amazing how many managers moan and whine about the demands on them, yet hold on tightly to interesting and fun tasks and projects that team members would enjoy. These managers miss the golden opportunity to increase team morale and energy by engaging team members in the organization's big picture.

3. **Be honest with top performers.** The essential corollary to ongoing involvement and recognition is the ongoing coaching about gaps in performance. High performers are not infallible and sometimes their areas for development involve interpersonal skills. Some high achievers can be prima donnas: they can forget to do essential paperwork, fail to say hello to other team members that they view as junior, and consider themselves too important to help clean up after a team potluck lunch. Or as we mentioned earlier, they can be deluded about their advancement potential, the compensation they should be paid, or the rules that apply to everyone.

    Whatever the challenges are in their behavior or performance, you are shortchanging both the individual and the team by ignoring them. In the short term, the person may be happier if they can get away with these gaps, but over time, the old adage, "What goes around, comes around" applies. Ongoing deviations between what an individual does and what the team expects will eventually poison the environment sufficiently to cause the team to fail good people, including the high performer.

4. **Help top performers achieve their career goals.** Managers often say, I just get the team fully staffed and operating well and somebody leaves! As the Buddhist faith points out, the acceptance of ongoing and perpetual change is the easiest route to feeling relaxed and peaceful. In other words, accept change as inevitable. Even before we can complete the creation of a team, its evolution (change), one way or another, is somewhere in the works. That's life, and it certainly applies to the workplace.

Rather than aspiring to build a permanent team, a more fruitful and rewarding goal may be to create a team environment that recruits wisely, has a strong and consistent process and structure to support ongoing success, and offers unique developmental opportunities.

That type of team—and the manager who runs it—develops a reputation as *the* place to work, one which is open to change and which supports career development and progression.

5. **Plan for the departure of top performers.** You must constantly be recruiting for great new people, including your top performers. While it is great to encourage people to stretch to their greatest potential, as the manager, you also need to plan for when the high performers move on. Expecting and planning for this to happen is a far better way to manage your team than resisting the team's evolution and trying to hold on to the current state forever.

How you watch for great potential team members depends on your business and industry. The best people to hire are usually those that you know by reputation, and you can only know people by getting out there and attending relevant seminars, trade shows, professional association meetings, social events, and gatherings within your own organization. You can also recruit from within your team. As people move up and out of your team, a positive message is conveyed by the promotion of a team member into the vacancy.

Change in the team—especially when the team is functioning well—may seem like the last thing you want to encourage. However, doing so is vitally important in managing top performers and it almost always brings fresh new ideas into the team. In the bigger picture, your role as a leader is to develop good people, not manage any particular team to infinity. Seen in this light, your long-term personal impact as a leader will be through the career development of high-potential individuals that cross your path for a time.

Some Personal Insights on Engaging High Performers

As well as engaging high performers through whatever avenues are open to you, we cannot repeat enough the importance of not taking them for granted. When an individual's successes and strengths become commonplace, it is very easy to stop noticing them and stop mentioning them, except maybe at the end of the year. We think, "Surely Jane knows how great I think she is! I have told her many times!" In fact, if she is like most people, Jane doesn't assume anything positive about her contribution unless feedback is consistently given to her.

The best feedback is very specific: rather than saying, "Great job!" as you pass in the hallway, helpful and rewarding feedback describes the specific positive outcome. An example is, "Jane, that presentation was fantastic. I could tell that the salespeople really liked the way you had a separate section on overcoming clients' objections. That was a great idea to include that piece."

SUMMING UP

Five key tips in managing top performers:

1. Keep them interested.
2. Spread the wealth of opportunities for developing a profile in the company.
3. Be honest.
4. Help them achieve their career goals.
5. Plan constantly for their departure.

Do It Yourself!

Opportunity 3: Managing Top Performers Effectively

- **Don't be mesmerized by people who are labeled as "stars."** Form your own opinions about people before accepting the corporate wisdom that someone can do no wrong. Sometimes people are granted the status of a top performer for the wrong reasons.
- **Look for diamonds in the rough.** A competitive advantage is available to your team if you find and develop people who are underestimated and who can be challenged to contribute more to the team. Look for ways to encourage and recognize them.
- **Be honest.** It is sometimes necessary to speak openly and candidly to make high performers aware of the gaps in their performance. If they really want to succeed quickly, they need to be delivering on all cylinders, including how they speak and behave, and the amount of time and effort they put into the job.
- **Encourage career progression for your top performers.** Don't hold people back because of a misguided desire to keep a great team intact. Look at the big picture and create a culture of growth and personal development. Know that in the long run, you will get ahead by being a place great people want to work, not one where change is a four letter word.
- **Recruit constantly.** The corollary to encouraging progression is replenishing the talent pool. Always think about people's next steps and who will succeed into their positions. Be involved in the industry and community so that you meet potential top talent. Keep in touch with former colleagues from other companies and roles, and

take time to have coffee with people who simply want to discuss their career with you. Over time these consistent connections provide your team with a range of options.

OPPORTUNITY 4

CONNECTING YOUR TEAM TO THE BIG PICTURE

Chapter 28

NO TEAM IS AN ISLAND

Real Life

Your biggest opportunities in leadership lie in the relationships you develop with your team, and the working relationships that you encourage and foster among the team members. There is no doubt that your leadership, combined with the right approach to your Plan, Process, and People can take your team a long way toward success.

However, another opportunity is yours for the taking: to develop and nurture relationships with the external and internal stakeholder networks *beyond* your team.

GIVING BACK

We have mentioned that encouraging your team members to seek out external feedback has several important benefits:

- Being receptive to ideas and suggestions from people outside the immediate team keeps your products and services fresh and competitive.
- Engaging the external marketplace gives ambitious team members opportunities to develop their communication skills.

- Hearing the demands of the marketplace firsthand helps your team understand the urgency of "getting it right."

But in addition to *receiving* feedback, you and your team also need to be communicating outwardly to the internal network, particularly your boss, your boss's boss, and peers and peer groups in your organization. These parties must:

- Know what your team is doing and be aware of its successes.
- Know what each individual does on the team and each individual's strengths and contributions.
- Think of your team not only as a successful team but also as a team that is pleasant and productive to work with, not "the Joint Ventures team from Hell on the 16th floor."

WHEN IT COMES TO REPUTATION, VISIBILITY IS EVERYTHING

Dispel any notions you have about "politics" and how it is beneath you to "suck up" to the boss. There is no need to be obsequious about managing your team's reputation internally, which is essential for these reasons:

- ***Boosting your team's visibility*** and by doing so, increasing its chance of getting access to any number of opportunities such as new capital investment, pilot projects, and additional staff.
- ***Defusing tough situations*** is essential before minor issues become a nightmare. For example, if you are regularly communicating with the compliance group about your team's challenges in getting a compliance procedure into place, the situation will be understood from the beginning rather than becoming a very unpleasant surprise uncovered by the corporate auditors.
- ***Ensuring that your team members are seen and appreciated*** for their good work leads to future opportunities for them. If this seems counterintuitive (Why would I want to let other

people see how great Sally is? Then I will lose her!), move on that outdated thinking. If Sally is so terrific, she will be moving on anyway. In the long run, it will be much better for team morale to be a champion of your team members' abilities.

- *Recruiting is simplified.* If you become known as a manager who doesn't take all the credit for success, but instead seeks out chances to speak highly of people on your team, recruitment of terrific new team members will become much easier.
- *You will have a better understanding of the expectations that are on your team.* Implicit in really understanding the Plan—a point we made in describing Responsibility 3—is knowing exactly what your boss and your boss's boss expect from your team. But we mention it again here because it is not a one-time discussion; regularly and consistently checking in to compare what you are doing with what your boss expects is fundamental to your team's success.

GETTING IT RIGHT WITH YOUR BOSS

How do you work more effectively with your boss to get the results you want for your team, your organization, and ultimately for yourself? This relationship is paramount to your success and also must be managed within your personal leadership style.

When thinking about your most important working relationships beyond your team, think first about your boss. He or she has the ability to make life for your team easy or difficult, and as the team leader, you are responsible for positioning your team in the best way. Your relationship with your boss is not only mutually dependent, but its effectiveness carries through to the success of your team.

BE ACCOUNTABLE ... TO THE RIGHT PERSON

When you take on a new leadership role, you need to quickly figure out to whom you are accountable. Maybe this will be crystal clear, because you only have one boss and everyone acknowledges that he or she calls the shots when it comes to your team's performance. But increasingly we seem to create ever more complicated organizational structures that make it hard to even know who "the boss" is.

Some organizational structures, such as the "matrix structure," insert one or two solid reporting lines here and a "dotted" line over there. Other places don't have particular names for how they are set up but nevertheless complicate who's who in the zoo. There are no foolproof guidelines for finding out whom you need to pay attention to, whose direction and ideas should be considered, and who should receive updates on your team's activities. Simply asking someone or assuming that the written organizational chart is accurate may not give you the whole picture. You will need to rely on your personal observation skills, likely over a period of time on the job.

No matter who your boss is, or how many bosses you may have, early on in your working relationship begin to gain a sense of the preferred style. Your manager's style includes factors such as frequency and formality of meetings between you; preferred format for information; hot buttons, or items or events that may be really irritating to him or her; and, of course, the actual and ongoing expectations of both you in the job and the results that are required from the team.

Some Personal Observations about Your Boss's Job

Try to always have a general awareness of what your boss has taken on as his responsibilities for the year and let him know those things being done by your team that coincide with the expectations on him. That isn't politics, it is just being smart! As long as your communications with your manager are about your team, not all about you, there is no downside to playing the "managing up" game.

It is naïve to think that what you and your team are doing well will necessarily be observed by anyone else. If you don't tell the people above you in the organization what's going on, rest assured that no one else is likely telling them. Sure, there is always an abundance of reports in organizations on a monthly, weekly, or even daily basis setting out the results, but you need to inform people at a different level, for example, about the activities that your team is doing to get its results.

If all of this sounds like too much time and effort for something not even on your job description, consider it from the perspective of being in your boss's shoes—what kind of information and updates would you find useful? Along the same lines, consider those people who are on your team and accountable to you—do all of them make being a boss very easy? Do some of them make being a manager very hard? In working with your boss, obviously you should emulate the people on your team who simplify your job, not make it worse. Your manager is human too, and your success in working with him or her not only helps you, it helps the team.

SUMMING UP

Just like the effort you put into any important relationship, getting to know your boss better just makes good sense. You want your boss to connect with you and to like working with you. Find out more about your boss's background and how he or she came to be in the position. It may also be useful to do the following:

1. Know what's negotiable and what's not.
2. Know what your boss's pet peeves and priorities are.
3. Observe and learn how your boss makes decisions.
4. Know when and how to approach your boss.
5. Submit reports once a week outlining your accomplishments—be brief, though!
6. Always stay positive—avoid negative emotions with your boss—your boss has his or her hands full. Empathy with your boss can go a long way. Until you and your manager

are on a firm footing, be respectful, polite, and formal in your communications at work. Be articulate and genuine.

7. Provide your boss with new ideas on a regular basis.

8. Accept and encourage your boss's feedback and concern for you.

9. Work in cooperation to achieve the Plan on time, every time, but be proactive about alerting your boss to any potential failures or mishaps. Believe it: your manager hates unpleasant surprises.

10. Take a no-surprises approach to deadlines. If you can't make them, be proactive about revising them. Then *make* the revised deadline.

11. Put yourself in your boss's shoes. Think in relation to his or her needs and then see if you can help. Stay away from passing judgment, unless you are specifically asked for this and then give reasons for your position.

12. Communicate with your boss in his or her preferred manner. If she prefers meeting by phone, schedule weekly phone meetings. If e-mail is most convenient, find out when he or she has uninterrupted thinking time, and if that's nine at night, make a habit of sending through your report then. You might just get a prompt, personal reply.

Above all, be a great follower: reliable, transparent, and trustworthy. Know what your boss is expecting of you and your team, and probe well to be clear. Ask for what you need to do your job.

Chapter 29

GETTING IT RIGHT WITH YOUR PEERS

Real Life

When you take on a new leadership assignment, you must quickly assess the People on your team, the Plan it has been handed to achieve, and the Process and structure that is in place.

The next thing to do is to figure out what you and your team need to do differently. Nine times out of ten at least some of these changes will require your team to ask for help and support from other parts of the organization. Perhaps your team's product line can only be delivered through retail channels of the larger organization or its delivery of merger and acquisition legal services only works if client groups ask for assistance early in the deal cycle. No matter what your team needs to do, it probably needs some help in getting done!

Your team's ability to get things done is largely dependent on its ability to effectively and appropriately ask for and receive help from partners.

> Reality? These partners can give you incomparable support and assistance, making your team shine, or they can throw roadblocks up all along the way, thwarting everything you try to do.

THE KEY TO SUCCESSFUL PEER GROUP RELATIONSHIPS IS THE RIGHT ATTITUDE

Enter into these relationships with an attitude of appreciation and an expectation that the relationship will be beneficial to both sides. Look the other way—once, twice, three times—when something goes sideways, and be a role model for professional peer relationships to your team. Although your success in working well with other parts of your organization is one part common sense and one part good attitude, some concrete ideas about how to forge these relationships include:

- *Invite members of other teams to attend your team meetings.* Your quarterly or offsite planning meetings are particularly good opportunities for your team to get to know their internal peers and partners better. Ask them to speak on a topic of interest in their area of expertise that impacts your team. For example, if you lead a marketing team, people from the frontline in sales would add invaluable insights to your deliberations on next year's strategy.

- *Get to know your peers on a more informal basis.* You can do this simply by making a point of attending organizational social events or by specifically including them in some of your team's events.

- *Make a point of understanding* their *priorities.* Instead of just focusing on what they can do for your team, how can your team help them? Understanding all of the expectations and demands placed on them by others in the company will also help you to establish a more efficient and effective working relationship.

- *Ask them for their views on their role with your team*: how they see themselves working with your team. You may have one idea about what you need from them, but perhaps they have other priorities that make your expectations unrealistic. Try to get to know your partners and their mandate early, before the demands of specific projects make communication and understanding more difficult.

- *Be considerate of their needs when working with them,* especially if you are asking for assistance. How much lead time do they need to help you out? In what format do they like to receive materials or requests?
- *Keep the lines of communication open* even once you are fully engaged with them on a number of specific matters. What else are they working on? What else are you and your team working on? Regularly try to rise above the day-to-day operational work you do together to talk about the bigger picture for each team.
- *Recognize their contributions.* Speak highly of the assistance other teams give to yours, and keep your difficulties between you and the other team leader.
- *Deal with problems early and directly,* keeping your discussions with the other manager at a professional and calm level. Aim to understand the situation and their perspective and don't rush to place blame. Keep the long-term relationship in mind at all times. *If you win a particular battle, will doing so hurt your teams' working relationship in the future?*

Do It Yourself!

Opportunity 4: Connecting Your Team to the Big Picture

- **Encourage the team to be receptive to information from the internal and external network.** Doing this increases the chance that the team will see trends and opportunities coming.

- **But also emphasize the importance of communicating what your team is doing and thinking.** In most cases, the details, and sometimes even the big picture, of what a work group is doing is not well known unless the manager makes a point of being an advocate for the team.

- **Don't say things like, "I don't play politics."** Every good manager owes it to the team to work at fostering strong relationships between the team and the manager's boss and other parts of the organization. That is not politics, just an astute awareness that wherever there are two or more people, issues of influence, communication, and plain old "getting along" will come up.

- **In communicating to the internal network, make it all about your team, not about you.** If you are the manager, for better or for worse, everybody knows you are responsible for the team and its results so don't say, "I did this" or "I did that." Look for ways to highlight what your team members accomplished.

- **Recognize that part of your job is to understand the internal corporate structure.** For your team's benefit, not to mention your own, you must know who your team is accountable to: *who do you need to keep informed?*

- **Every boss has one or two key characteristics that you need to know.** Perhaps your manager's style includes a desire for detailed reports to be prepared before every meeting or an aversion to e-mail. Figure these out.

- **Make great internal relationships a priority.** Find out early and often what is going on with the teams that work with your team, and don't adopt a stance of being demanding or insistent that your priorities come first.

CONCLUSION

The pace of change has everyone working furiously and not always in tandem for the same results. It's enough, at the end of yet another long day of people and process problems, to make you sigh: "They Just Don't Get it!"

The role of middle management has re-emerged as a critical factor in the success of companies who want to increase productivity from their employees and lead in their markets. The team development seen as a central part of your job is acknowledged as the only way ever-increasing productivity targets can be met.

When it comes to "self-help books" for managers, it is common to find two main themes. The first theme is high-level strategy, setting out a new focus or vision that will take the company to the next level of success, enabling the company to keep up with the relentless demands for higher revenue and profit each year.

The second common theme in management books is more around "style," the required managerial interpersonal skills, the nature of the conversations, the finessing of team dynamics and the defusing of conflict. All of these books are tremendously helpful.

Middle managers need to consider both sides of the equation-the aggressive results required and also the high expectations people now have about their jobs. Targets can't be missed in the short term, it's true, but the human need to have meaning in one's work must be fulfilled over the long haul. Failure on either points can bring a leader down.

To excel, the astute manager must become a team leader. Rather than separating the head office's aggressive business plan from the requests from employees for more working flextime, we've suggested that both demands are part of an ongoing conversation among the individuals on the team. By having a process in place to understand and assimilate the business plan, and a commitment to really knowing and understanding the people on the team, you can achieve the results demanded today of all leaders.

Furthermore, we believe that if a leadership role is creating ongoing, debilitating stress for you, then there is something wrong. In our experience, the most successful leaders are often those who are the least stressed out, whereas those managers who are constantly tired and worried may be underachieving due to their consistent toleration of what are really intolerable behaviors or attitudes.

To get the results you want and need, you must establish a structure within which to manage a talented, complementary team of individuals, in an open and transparent process, that exceeds the expectations of your essential stakeholders.

A team managed by an accountable, bold, caring, and detached leader can and *should* be personally rewarding—even with the demands of our 24/7 global marketplace.

> "He who every morning plans the transactions of the day and follows out that plan, carries a thread that will guide him through the labyrinth of the most busy life."
>
> Victor Hugo

BIBLIOGRAPHY

Baker, Stephen and Heather Green. "Blogs Will Change Your Business." *Business Week*, 02 May, 2005: 57–67.

Baldoni, John. "The Presence of Leadership." 04 Aug, 2005 *Darwin Magazine*. 08 Jan, 2006 <http://www2.darwinmag.com/read/feature/aug05_baldoni.cfm>.

Blanchard, Kenneth and Spencer Johnson. *The One Minute Manager*. New York: William Morrow and Company, Inc., 1982.

Canadian Business and Waterstone Human Capital Ltd. "2005 Canadian Corporate Culture Study." Fall 2005. 12 Jan, 2006 <www.waterstonehc.com/resources/Culture.pdf>.

Charan, Ram and Geoffrey Colvin. "Why CEO's Fail." *Fortune* 139 (21 June, 1999): 68–78.

Conger, J.A. and R.N. Kanungo. *Charismatic Leadership in Organizations*. Thousand Oaks: Sage Publications, 1998.

Conway, N. and David Guest. *Employee Well-Being and the Psychological Contract*. London: Chartered Institute of Personnel and Development, 2004.

Covey, Stephen. *First Things First Every Day*. New York: Fireside, 1997.

De Pree, Max. "Creative Leadership." *Leader to Leader* Vol. 20 (Spring 2001): 10–13.

Drucker, Peter F. *The Effective Executive*. New York: Harper Business, 1993.

Duxbury, L. and Christopher Higgins. *Who is at Risk? Predictors of Work-Life Conflict (Report Four)*. Ottawa: Public Health Agency, 2005.

Galt, Virginia. "Employers Search for Fountain of Youth." *The Globe & Mail* 10 Aug, 2005: C1.

Galt, Virginia. "Lousy People Skills Are Biggest Hurdle for Leaders." *Globe & Mail* 15 Oct, 2005: B11.

Goldsmith, Kelly and Marshall Goldsmith. "Why Coaching Clients Give Up— And How Effective Goal Setting Can Make a Positive Difference." Nov 2005, *Link & Learn*. 08 Jan, 2006 <http://www.linkageinc.com/company/news_events/link_learn_enewsletter/archive/2005/11_05_coaching_goldsmith.aspx>.

Goleman, Daniel. *Emotional Intelligence*. New York: Bantam Books, 1995.

Gray, Jim. "Five Words That Can Make All the Difference." *The Globe & Mail*, 21 July, 2004: C3.

Gray, Jim. "Showing Class Can Boost Career Potential." *National Post's Financial Post*, 12 Oct, 2005: WK3.

Greene, Robert. *The 48 Laws of Power*. New York: Penguin Books, 2000.

Greenleaf, Robert K. *Servant Leadership: A Journey into the Nature of Legitimate Power and Greatness (25th Anniversary Edition)*. Ed. Larry C. Spears. New York: Paulist Press, 2002.

Gwynne, Peter. "Top Employers Survey." *Science*, Vol. 309 (30 Sept, 2005): 2237–2250.

Hawkins, John. "Principled Leadership in an Age of Cynicism." April 1997 *Positive Impact*. 10 Jan, 2006 <http://www.leadershiplifestyle.com/articles/april97.htm>.

Immen, Wallace. "The New Game Plan: Top-To-Bottom Coaching." *Globe & Mail*, 14 Sept, 2005: C1.

Izzo, John B. and Pam Withers. *Values Shift*. Toronto: Prentice Hall, 2000.

Kushner, Harold. *When All You've Ever Wanted Isn't Enough*. New York: Simon & Schuster, Fireside, 2002.

Lai, Tim. "A Wise Boss Is Also a Good Samaritan." *Globe & Mail*, 02 Sept, 2005: C1.

Lawford, G. Ross. *The Quest for Authentic Power*. San Francisco: Berrett-Koehler Publishers, Inc., 2002.

Mayo, Anthony J. and Nitin Nohria. *In Their Time: The Greatest Business Leaders of the Twentieth Century*. Boston: Harvard Business School Press, 2005.

Merchant, Kenneth A. *Rewarding Results, Harvard Business School Series in Accounting and Control*. Boston: Harvard Business School Press, 1989.

Morris, Betsy. "Genentech: The Best Place to Work Now." 20 Jan, 2006, *CNN Money*. 22 Jan 2006 <http://money.cnn.com/2006/01/06/news/companies/bestcos_genentech/index.htm>. http://money.cnn.com/services/terms.html.

Musser, S.J. *The Determination of Positive and Negative Charismatic Leadership*. Unpublished Manuscript, Grantham, PA: Messiah College, 1987.

Newmont Mining Corporation. "Vision and Values." 2004 *Newmont Mining Corporation*. 18 Jan, 2006 <http://www.newmont.com/en/about/vision/index.asp>.

Novak, Michael. *Business as a Calling*. New York: Free Press, 1996.

Reisman, Heather. Acceptance Speech. Asper School of Business: International Distinguished Entrepreneur Award. Winnipeg Convention Centre, Winnipeg. 05 June, 2003.

Robert, Michel. *Product Innovation Strategy*. New York: McGraw-Hill, 1995.

Rubin, Sander. "Mensa: 1973 Annual Report." *Mensa Bulletin*, May 1973.

Secretan, Lance. "Shelve Processes, Share Experiences." 12 Oct, 1998, *Industry Week*. 10 Jan, 2006 <http://66.102.7.104/search?q=cache:wcZslC8oTU0J:www.industry week.com/IWGC/columns.asp%3FColumnId%3D219>.

Stern, Michael. "If You Want to Be the CEO, Expect to Put in the Hours." *The National Post's Financial Post*, 18 June, 2005: FW9.

Tesolin, Arupa. "Five Ways to Invite Intuition to Your Training Session." 2002 *Intuita*, 22 Jan, 2006 <http://www.intuita.com/articles10.htm>.

INDEX

INDEX

ABOUT THE AUTHORS

JEAN BLACKLOCK, B.COMM., LL.B

Jean Blacklock is the Chief Operating Officer of BMO Trust Company and the Vice President and Managing Director of Personal Trust Services for BMO Harris Private Banking, part of the BMO Financial Group.

She is a graduate of the University of Saskatchewan in Saskatoon, Saskatchewan, Canada, where she pursued the combined Commerce-Law program, attaining a Bachelor of Commerce degree (Accounting major) in 1984 and Bachelor of Laws in 1985. Upon graduation, Jean articled in law in Calgary, Alberta, becoming a member of the Law Society of Alberta in 1986. In 1994, Jean was admitted to the partnership of the Howard, Mackie law firm (now Borden Ladner Gervais LLP) where she led the wills and estates group.

In 1998, Jean was appointed as an executive of BMO Financial Group. Until 2003, Jean was Vice President and Managing Director, BMO Harris Private Banking, Prairies, where she led a team of professionals across the three Prairie provinces, providing private banking, trust and investment services to high net worth individuals. In 2003, Jean was appointed to her current executive position as Chief Operating Officer of BMO Trust Company, and Vice President, Personal Trust Services, BMO Harris Private Banking, based in Toronto.

Jean wrote a column on estate planning from 1994 to 2000 for the *Calgary Herald* (syndicated for Southam newspapers) and in 2001, co-authored a book with Susan Murphy and Judy Miyashiro on estate planning called *Food for Thought: Bringing Estate Planning to Life* (John Wiley & Sons, Canada).

Jean is the author of The Knowledge Bureau Course entitled "The Empathetic Advisor: Strategic Purpose in Estate Planning."

In June 2004, Jean joined the Board of Directors of the Canadian Breast Cancer Foundation, Ontario Chapter, for which she is currently the Vice-Chair.

EVELYN JACKS

Evelyn Jacks is an award-winning entrepreneur, a consistently best-selling author, speaker, educator, and publisher in the tax preparation and financial services industries. She is well known to millions as the leading resource on open-line shows for help in answering the tax questions average Canadians need answers to. Her trademark style is one of simplicity for an enormously complex subject to help Canadians reduce the taxes they pay.

Evelyn's companies have specialized in publishing continuing education for professional tax and financial advisors for over 25 years. Evelyn is the founder and president of The Knowledge Bureau, Canada's leading continuing education provider in the tax and financial services industry. The company is home of the Distinguished Financial Advisor (DFA) Certificate CE and Designation Programs. It is also a leading source of interpretive news to media and Canada's leading financial speaker's bureau.

The Knowledge Bureau has recently partnered with the Schulich Executive Education Centre, rated number 1 in the world in public programming, to offer both the DFA designation and a Masters Certificate in Tax or Investment Services to successful financial advisors. The Knowledge Bureau also produces, hosts and delivers the Distinguished Advisor Conference, an annual national education conference for tax and financial advisors.

Evelyn is one of Canada's most prolific national authors and publishers. She has written 36 books on the subject of personal taxation, as well as published over 100 certificate vocational courses on the subject of tax, tax accounting, tax planning, and business practices for tax accountants and financial planners.

Evelyn is an internationally recognized, award-winning entrepreneur, several times over. In 1986, Evelyn Jacks' selection as the YM-YWCA "Business Woman of the Year" recognized her significant contributions to the community in establishing a national profile for tax preparation and tax planning services.

In 1997 Evelyn won Manitoba's Entrepreneur of the Year award. Later that year, she won the prestigious Rotman School of Business National Canadian Entrepreneur of the Year Award in Toronto. In 1998 she was recognized with an International Business Leadership Award by the Canadian Embassy in Washington, D.C. In 1999, she was appointed by the Premier of Manitoba to be a Commissioner for the Lower Tax Commission.

Evelyn has maintained significant influence in the national media through her years as a highly respected featured commentator on tax policy in newspapers and on radio and television. She has written thousands of articles and analysis for numerous papers and magazines and for several industry Internet portals, specializing in tax, tax planning, and tax practice management. In November 2005 she was chosen as The Winnipeg Free Press's Inspiring Woman.

Currently Evelyn is active in a number of volunteer leadership positions including Governor of the Manitoba Club, where she sits on the Cabinet of the Capital Campaign and as Chair of the Communications Committee. Evelyn is also a member of the Board of Associates at the University of Manitoba, with leadership of the Communications Committee, and she is a Cabinet Member of the United Way of Winnipeg.